ALONE IN
PLAIN SIGHT

Praise for *Alone in Plain Sight*

"In *Alone in Plain Sight* Ben shows the world what made him a good Bachelor, but more importantly, what makes him a great man and even better friend. Ben is fearlessly vulnerable, open, and honest in this book about his own struggles in order to help us all grow together. Now, more than ever, we need words like these to help us find connection instead of division, common ground instead of a battleground. Ben understands life is complicated and needs and deserves more than just a positive quote on social media."

—Chris Harrison, host of ABC's hit romance reality
franchise *The Bachelor* and *The Bachelorette*

"Ben's ability to look at the world through a lens of curiosity, vulnerability, and hope is what makes *Alone in Plain Sight* a must-read for anyone looking to reconnect to themselves, others, and the One who knows us best."

—Bob Goff, author of three *New York Times* bestsellers:
Love Does; Everybody, Always; and *Dream Big*

"There are books you enjoy. There are books that make you think. Then there are books that force you to be honest. Ben, in *Alone in Plain Sight*, has forced us to be honest with ourselves. He forces us to ask what's missing, what are we searching for, what can we appreciate, and what can we imagine that will be better for us? In this brilliant and beautifully written book, Ben dares us to find meaning in both the compelling and complex parts of our stories. He invites us to sit still, be calm, and wonder. He charts his emotional life, his personal struggles, his journey with God, and experience of love. More than anything, Ben invites us to be more human. That's what it is, that is what makes this special and worth our time: to read this book is to become more human. Embraced. Connected. Loved. Seen."

—Dante Stewart, writer and host

"To all those searching for true connection: you're in good company! *Alone in Plain Sight* by my friend, Ben Higgins, is tackling some of life's biggest questions and giving them true, hopeful, and applicable answers. I'm personally thankful for Ben's reminder that we've always been seen, loved, and never alone."

—Sadie Robertson Huff, author, speaker, and founder of Live Original

"Vulnerable, transparent, and honest Ben Higgins takes us into his struggles that echo so surprisingly like the ones all of us experience. But in *Alone in Plain Sight* he doesn't just leave us there. We get to grow right alongside him as, over time, he learns to find his identity in the One that matters most."

—Tyler Merritt, creator of the Tyler Merritt Project

"Ben Higgins has been able to use his platform to help so many through his charity work, mission projects, and now through *Alone in Plain Sight*. For people who are feeling lonely, yearning for a sense of belonging, and in need of a safe place to be vulnerable, this book will help inspire you to bravely make connections and build communities. If you feel like you need a friend, Ben Higgins will be just that as you read this book. He understands what you're feeling; you're not alone in feeling alone. As discussed in the book, we may be living in one of the most isolated times in history—retreating to your safe space may be comfortable and the desire to detach from those with different viewpoints can be tempting. However, *Alone in Plain Sight* explains how much more fulfilled we will be with our lives if we exit our comfort zones and communicate with open minds and hearts."

—Ashley Iaconetti Haibon and Jared Haibon

"In *Alone in Plain Sight* Ben Higgins takes what is already known of his public life and adds the personal, deeper things—the questions and stories of God, others, and himself—and it creates a book that is honest, relatable, generous, and encouraging. I finished reading it and felt, somehow, less alone in my life too."

—Annie F. Downs, bestselling author and host of *That Sounds Fun* podcast

"Ben Higgins has many aspirational qualities, but his genuine intellectual curiosity is the one I envy most. While many people assume they know the world they live in, Ben is on a constant quest for understanding. I've never met anyone I enjoyed disagreeing with more, as those disagreements always led to empathy and betterment on both sides. In a world where morality seems harder and harder to find, I truly consider Ben a diamond in the rough, an embodiment of non-performative kindness. *Alone in Plain Sight* is less of a how-to and more of an unvarnished self-exploration, an attempt to reconcile what life is with what life could be. I encourage you to read it, especially if you think you have nothing to learn from him."

—Elan Gale, television producer and author of *You're Not That Great*

"I once heard a wise man say, 'There are two things in life that make the world go round—money and relationships. Only one of those will make you rich, and it's not money.' Nothing is more fundamental to the human experience than the relationships we form and Ben understands this as well as anyone I've ever met. I love this book because it captures the essence of who Ben is: authentic, honest, vulnerable, wise, and someone who is marked by his love for God and people. I promise you are going to love this book, from the amazing stories of people that he's crossed paths with to the incredible nuggets of wisdom that he weaves in and out of each chapter. I hope you enjoy it as much as I did!"

—Chad Bruegman, pastor, conference speaker, and executive coach

"Life is hard. We all fall short, we compare ourselves to others, and we've all felt rejection, regret, or loneliness. *Alone in Plain Sight* offers heartfelt stories, introspective questions, and biblical references to guide each of us on our own journey to feeling understood, relatable, and heard. After reading this book, I have confidence that life is meant to be done together and I'm never alone as I face adversity!"

—Cody Zeller, former Indiana University basketball player and current player in the NBA

"Honest, vulnerable, humble, full of kindness and love, this book is a direct reflection of who Ben Higgins is as a human. A constant example of how to love others—*Alone in Plain Sight* exemplifies God's love through Ben's words."

—Becca Tilley, host of the *Scrubbing In* podcast

"No matter what season of life you are in, this book (and Ben) will make you feel less alone on your journey. Ben's beautiful heart and faith shine so bright. I feel lucky to be part of this community and continue to learn from Ben's heart for people."

—Tanya Radisavljevic, radio, podcast, and tv personality

"As Ben's friend and pastor, *Alone in Plain Sight* reminds me of why I love how he has used his platform for good. It is a joy for me to see growth and depth in Ben. My hope for you is that as you read this book you will be blessed as I was as you get to peer into life more fully and get to know Ben a little bit better."

—Denny Wilson, pastor of Warsaw Community Church

"A beautifully written exploration of spirituality, human relationships, and how our childhoods affect us. I love seeing Ben's heart of gold shine."

—Sarah Boyd, Ben's manager and vice president of business development at Socialyte

ALONE IN PLAIN SIGHT

Searching for Connection When You're Seen But Not Known

BEN HIGGINS

WITH MARK TABB

NELSON
BOOKS

An Imprint of Thomas Nelson

Alone in Plain Sight

Published in Nashville, Tennessee, by Nelson Books, an imprint of Thomas Nelson. Nelson Books and Thomas Nelson are registered trademarks of HarperCollins Christian Publishing, Inc.

Thomas Nelson titles may be purchased in bulk for educational, business, fundraising, or sales promotional use. For information, please email SpecialMarkets@ThomasNelson.com.

Unless otherwise noted, Scripture quotations are taken from the Holy Bible, New Living Translation. Copyright © 1996, 2004, 2015 by Tyndale House Foundation. Used by permission of Tyndale House Publishers, Inc., Carol Stream, Illinois 60188. All rights reserved.

Scripture quotations marked AMP are taken from the Amplified Bible. Copyright © 1954, 1958, 1962, 1964, 1965, 1987, 2015 by the Lockman Foundation, La Habra, California 90631. All rights reserved.

Scripture quotations marked THE MESSAGE are taken from *THE MESSAGE.* Copyright © 1993, 2002, 2018 by Eugene H. Peterson. Used by permission of NavPress. All rights reserved. Represented by Tyndale House Publishers, Inc.

Scripture quotations marked NIV are taken from The Holy Bible, New International Version®, NIV®. Copyright © 1973, 1978, 1984, 2011 by Biblica, Inc.® Used by permission of Zondervan. All rights reserved worldwide. www.Zondervan.com.

Any internet addresses, phone numbers, or company or product information printed in this book are offered as a resource and are not intended in any way to be or to imply an endorsement by Thomas Nelson, nor does Thomas Nelson vouch for the existence, content, or services of these sites, phone numbers, companies, or products beyond the life of this book.

ISBN 978-1-4002-3093-8 (signed)
ISBN 978-1-4002-2140-0 (TP)
ISBN 978-1-4002-5642-6 (expanded edition)

Library of Congress Cataloging-in-Publication Data

Names: Higgins, Ben, 1989- author. | Tabb, Mark A., author.
Title: Alone in plain sight : searching for connection when you're seen but not known / Ben Higgins with Mark Tabb.
Description: Nashville, Tennessee : Nelson Books, [2021] | Includes bibliographical references. | Summary: "The cofounder of Generous Coffee and lead of The Bachelor's twentieth season reveals the key to being seen and known, as well as to leading a life that truly matters"-- Provided by publisher.
Identifiers: LCCN 2020033207 | ISBN 9781400221356 (hardcover) | ISBN 9781400221363 (epub)
Subjects: LCSH: Loneliness--Religious aspects--Christianity. | Christian life. | Identity (Psychology)--Religious aspects--Christianity.
Classification: LCC BV4911 .H53 2021 | DDC 248.8/6--dc23 LC record available at https://lccn. loc.gov/2020033207

Printed in the United States of America
25 26 27 28 29 LBC 5 4 3 2 1

I dedicate this book to the teachers, family members, loved ones, friends, and strangers who have helped shape my story. Specifically, thank you to my mom, Amy, and my dad, Dave, for being constant friends and leaders in my life.

To Jessica, I love you. You have loved me through my best and worst, and you still stand by my side.

To my Lord Jesus who has never let me go— even in the midst of my greatest confusion, doubt, and wrestling, you have stayed near.

Contents

A Personal Note from Ben

A few years ago I sat down to write a book I hoped might help the reader feel less alone. My desire has always been to create space in this disorienting, chaotic, defeating, and lonely world that allows struggling humans (which is all of us) to see some light shining in the darkness. I personally believe there is a God who has called us into lives that are so much more beautiful, so much more connected, and so much more joy-filled than the ones we're living now.

Fortunately, or unfortunately depending on your point of view, *Alone in Plain Sight* was released in the heart of the global pandemic. I say "fortunately" because I think at the time people needed a book about human connection more than ever. Unfortunately, the pandemic meant the book and media tour were cancelled. I had planned to travel across the United States meeting you, my readers, in bookstores and coffee shops and listening to your stories. Instead, I found myself sitting on a couch, watching my email, hoping that anyone who read the book would reach out. People did reach out, and it led to some fantastic conversations that I cherish, but somehow the experience felt more disconnected than connected.

I could blame the pandemic for what I feel it took from me and from so many of you. I could get sad about not being able to meet you in person. But instead I choose to be excited to re-release this book with new additions recounting some of the events that have happened in my life during the past five years, including getting married to the most amazing human on the planet, Jessica Clarke. As one country song says, "I am not an easy man to love," but thank goodness Jessica continues to love me. For that I am grateful. We also welcomed a beautiful baby girl into this world on February 12, 2025. Winona Elane Higgins came into our lives and forever changed us. As I write this note she is learning to smile and screech (we call it singing) and discovering that she has hands. I could write a whole book on what love feels like after just a few short weeks with Winona, but I will summarize it by saying that I did not know a heart could be stretched to hold this much love, hope, joy, and care. And that connecting to another human being could have so much depth.

Yes, a lot has happened since *Alone in Plain Sight* first published. In all honesty, the last few years have felt like a fever dream. And yet, despite all the growth that has come from years of therapy, contemplation, and prayer, I still have times when I feel like an outsider, like no one understands me, like I am the kid who wasn't invited to the party and is standing on the outside looking in. I still struggle with these emotions, but I have developed tools to speak truth into my life.

Through this book I have connected with incredible humans who also struggle with these emotions and, as a result, I feel less alone. In short, life has not stopped for me, and new lessons arise every day to better myself. So, as I did when I first put words to paper, I pray that those who read this book will feel less alone and more connected. I also pray that Winona can read it one day and know her dad better. So this book is for you, the reader, and also for my family, whom I love so much.

Here's to you and this journey,

Introduction

ON THE OUTSIDE LOOKING IN

Back in grade school, recess was my favorite part of the day. Reading class came in a close second, especially when Mrs. B, the librarian, read to us. Those times became few and far between as we got old enough to read on our own, but they still happened often enough in second grade that we could continue to hope today might be the day.

Our hopes came true one afternoon when Mrs. B announced, "Okay, everybody down into the reading pit." She always read a book to us when we went down into the reading pit. I just hoped it might be one of my favorites. Mrs. B had other plans.

Once we were all seated in the pit, she said, "Today we're going to do partner reading." Even though none of us had any idea what she meant by partner reading, we all started bouncing up and down like it was Christmas morning. "Everyone find a reading buddy, and the two of you will go back and forth reading to each other," Mrs. B continued. "You can team up with *anyone* you want. Now find a partner and get started."

All at once the entire class jumped up and started running around, tagging partners. The library became joyful chaos, and I was happily in the middle of it all. I looked around for a moment, spotted a friend, then darted over to him. However, before I got there someone else tagged my friend as their partner. No big deal. I had lots of friends. Everyone in class was my friend, so onto the next I ran!

But my next friend already had a partner too. And so did the next and the next and the next, until it hit me that everyone in the class had a reading partner—everyone but me. Our teacher had not yet taught us about even and odd numbers, but I learned about them the hard way that day. I was the odd man out. I never imagined this could happen to me.

Dejected, I wandered over to the corner of the room and slumped down in a seat. Mrs. B came over and said, "Well, Ben, you can be *my* partner today," in that perky voice adults use when they're trying to cheer you up without sounding like they're trying to cheer you up. When you're on the receiving end, the words sound pretty hollow.

"Okay," I said with a forced smile. I got up, grabbed a book, and followed Mrs. B to her desk. It felt like the walk of shame, like everyone in my class was staring at me, the loner kid who got stuck with the teacher as his reading partner because he didn't have any friends. Looking back, I doubt if anyone even noticed who my partner was, but I did. I felt like the charity case, the outsider, the one who had a lot of "friends" who were really just acquaintances and were nice to me only because they had to be. Looking back, I doubt if anyone else actually felt that way about me, but I did and that was enough.

That feeling stuck with me long after the second grade. For most of my life I've felt like an outsider, like the kid who never gets invited to the party but is stuck looking in through the window while everyone else has a great time without him. I'm not suggesting I'd be a completely different person if someone would have picked me as their reading partner when I was in second grade. But when I walked into school on the first day of kindergarten, I already had a deep fear of being rejected by peers. As an only child, I spent most of my childhood surrounded by adults, not kids my age. I never knew what was hot or cool, and kids made fun of me because of it. Carrying on a conversation with one of my parents' friends came a lot more easily than talking about Pokémon with another kid on the playground.

My mom and dad never intended for me to be an only child. They spent four long years working with infertility specialists just to have me. Then, five months into my mother's pregnancy, she developed a severe placenta previa hemorrhage. Her doctor put her in the hospital because she ran the risk of bleeding out. On top of that, two months after my parents discovered I was on the way, my dad was diagnosed with stage four Hodgkin's lymphoma. At one point both of my parents were in the hospital at the same time. Thankfully, both survived, but between the complications from my mom's pregnancy and the toll the severe chemo and radiation therapies took on my dad, they weren't having any more children.

After their brushes with death, my parents were never the same. They counted every day as precious. From as far back as I can remember, both of them taught me to approach each day as a gift from God. The belief that every day matters, as does every person in my life, was instilled in me throughout childhood. My parents made sure nothing was ever left unsaid—to me, one another, friends, or extended family. Staying connected with the people they loved gave weight to every relationship in their lives. Growing up, I assumed such a thoughtful approach to life and relationships was the norm. I thought every family lived this way. Little did I know that my family was an exception.

Once I started school, I dove into friendships with the same kind of earnestness I experienced at home. I didn't know there was such a thing as a casual acquaintance. Friends were friends, and we stuck with one another no matter what. When no one picked me to be their reading partner, I felt more than left out. I jumped to feeling genuine rejection, embarrassment, and confusion. Personal connections ran deep with me. How could people I believed to be my friends just throw our relationship to the side? What if they never saw me as a friend at all? What if every relationship was all a facade?

I never felt like I completely fit in. No one had to tell me I was different. I believed it, and that was enough. Being rejected by every kid in my class on the same day in second grade only confirmed what I already believed to be true about myself. From that day on I began living out a self-fulfilling prophecy. I created a narrative inside my own head that told me I was not seen, not heard, not valued. I was alone in plain sight. If I ever started to doubt it, life came along and confirmed my worst fears.

Confirming the Worst

Back in college I roomed with three guys who played on the Indiana University basketball team. If you are reading this and live outside of Indiana, let me tell you that playing for IU isn't like playing for just any college basketball team. Around there they have a saying that goes, "In forty-nine other states it's just basketball. But this is Indiana!"

All through junior high and high school I dreamed of one day playing for the Hoosiers. Like most other kids I knew, when I shot baskets in my driveway, I imagined I was taking the last-second shot in the NCAA finals for the national title. Sometimes I made it. Sometimes I missed. But I hoped someday my dream could come true.

I didn't just pursue my dream in my driveway. In addition to playing on my junior high and high school teams, I played on a top-ten nationally ranked Amateur Athletic Union traveling team. Every guy on that team ended up playing Division I ball—every guy but one. Me. I hurt my knee my junior year and two surgeries later my dreams of playing college ball were crushed. To be honest, the chances of me actually landing a Division I scholarship were pretty slim, much less being recruited by IU, but some of my friends made it. That's how I ended up rooming with three IU basketball players and becoming friends with some other guys on the team, some of whom went on to play in the NBA.

My friends and I were close. However, every time we went somewhere together, the feeling of not fitting in came crawling back over me. My friends never did anything to make me feel out of place. They didn't have to. Other people took care of that.

Almost every time we went somewhere in the state of Indiana, IU basketball fans would come to our table, bubbling over with adoration, and say, "Oh my gosh, I can't believe it's you. Can I take a selfie with you guys?" When the fans got to me, they'd give me a look as if they were googling the team roster in their heads, trying to figure out who I was. Eventually they'd ask, "So, who are you?"

"Nobody," I always answered.

Then why would these stars hang out with you? I could feel them wondering. *You don't belong here.* No one ever actually told me I didn't deserve to hang out with the basketball gods of Indiana. They didn't have to. The looks on their faces said it all. I couldn't argue the point. I didn't belong. My friends were athletes. I was the dud who stayed back at our apartment, eating pizza, drinking beer, and binge-watching movies while they were at practice. In a word, I was the outsider. I didn't fit in, so why try?

Not Alone?

I never imagined anyone else felt the same way I did. Maybe that's part of life as an outsider. Your mind won't let you believe you fit in anywhere, even if you find others who feel exactly the same way as you. The wounds from all the self-fulfilling prophecies of rejection that reinforce feelings of being unloved and unwanted lock you into a destructive mindset where you can never fit in. That's where I was. In my mind, everyone else fit in somewhere. Everyone else was in on the joke while I stood outside the circle thinking the joke was on me. I could never see myself as anything other than the odd man out, and it ate at me more than I wanted to admit.

And then something odd happened.

I found myself on *The Bachelorette*, along with twenty-four other guys, hoping to connect with one girl. As the weeks went by, the number of guys kept dwindling as Kaitlyn sent one after another home. But she kept me around. Eventually the number of guys pursuing the girl dropped down into single digits. Toward the end of the show's run, I found myself alone with this girl and, for the first time in my life, I opened up about the feelings I'd carried around since Mrs. B's reading class experience. However, rather than saying I felt like an outsider, I told her I felt unlovable, like no one would ever get me. She didn't really get me either, because she sent me home a couple of episodes later. I wasn't surprised. I could hardly believe I lasted as long as I did. Her rejection only confirmed my outsider feelings even more.

I wasn't really thinking about the cameras when I opened up to this girl. The moment felt very private, like it was just between the two of us. Of course, it wasn't. A few months later the entire world (or at least the fans of the show) watched my moment of vulnerability play out, complete with added background music. Then something very surprising happened. Right after the episode aired, people started sending me messages through my social media accounts and through the television network. My words must have connected with all the outsiders out there, because one person after another wrote to tell me that they, too, struggled with feeling unlovable. Somehow, my confession of my own insecurities and failures made them feel connected to me, like I was someone safe they could open up to.

The messages kept coming and coming. People walked up to me in airports and at ball games and wherever I went, thanking me for what I said and telling me their own stories of feeling like they did not fit in. The response was so great that I began to wonder if I had stumbled onto something.

Perhaps most of us feel like outsiders. Maybe there are more of us standing outside in the rain, staring in at the party we'll never be invited to, than there are those inside. I wasn't exactly sure what to do with this idea, but it eventually became clear in the unlikeliest of places.

Most Divisive Time in History?

In 2018 I was invited to speak at a political conference and share the story of a coffee company I cofounded, where I serve as president. Generous International is a for-purpose company dedicated to contributing profits to social causes around the world. I came to the conference to talk about the potential impact of socially responsible companies that fight injustice around the world. Going in, I felt more than a little intimidated by the impressive roster of speakers this conference brought together. When it came to social justice and politics, this conference truly was a who's who.

All of the speakers were former heads of state, senators, governors, powerful attorneys, and university elites, while I was just a guy who became semi-famous for appearing on a reality television show. The organizers also allowed me to set up a booth to serve coffee during the event, which gave me plenty of opportunities to listen to the sessions and engage in conversations with some of our nation's finest.

During one of the sessions, a well-intentioned student passionately argued that we are now living in *the* most divisive time in United States history. I've heard this statement many times before, everywhere from news analysts to social media posts. Most of the time I don't over-analyze it. I know what the speakers are trying to say. Like many of us, they are alarmed at the toxicity of every political discussion today. I started to file the student's comments away into the same mental file I go to every time I hear this comment, but before I could, one of my best friends leaned over and whispered, "That doesn't feel right, does it?"

The more I thought about it, the more convinced I became that my friend was right. The Civil War obviously was a more divided time than now. Looking back at human history, I don't know that we've ever been very united, in the United States or anywhere else in the world. Humanity dreams of peace, but that dream never comes true. The history of the world is filled with wars and genocide and oppression.

Yet, as I thought about how often I hear people say we now live in *the* most divisive time in history, I realized people do feel something unlike anything they've felt in the past. I then asked myself if this *something* might be related to all the messages I still receive in the wake of my national television confession. It feels like every day someone writes to tell me how they feel lonely and insufficient. Could this be what we are collectively feeling? Have we become a nation of outsiders, feeling cut off and separated from one another? I don't think we live in the most divisive time in history, but it certainly seems like we are feeling more isolated and lonely than ever before.

The numbers back this up. According to a recent Harvard study, 40 percent of people admit to a deep-seated feeling of loneliness or isolation. This number has doubled over the last twenty years, even as social networks and social media have exploded.[1] How can this be? The researchers found that loneliness is contagious, like the coronavirus, and can actually be deadly. Living an isolated life produces the same kind of health problems one might find in someone who smokes fifteen cigarettes a day—including heart disease and strokes.[2] That means loneliness is literally killing us. We may also be killing one another with it. Researchers have found that human beings push the lonely out of the group and into the fringes, which mirrors my experience. We start out feeling socially isolated, but that push from the "connected" leaves us physically isolated.[3]

I believe isolation and divisiveness go hand in hand. The stronger our feelings of standing outside the main group, the more we withdraw into ourselves and only listen to the voices of those who reinforce our isolation. We end up living in little silos. If we connect with others, we only connect with those who see the world the way we see it and think the way we think and fear the same things we fear. Before long we begin to look with suspicion on anyone outside our silo. An us-against-them mindset sinks in, more out of fear than anything else. The walls of the silos keep getting higher and higher, and those invited in become fewer and fewer, leaving us even more isolated, which makes the vicious cycle spin even faster.

The story doesn't have to end there, which is why I am writing this book. I don't pretend to have all the answers, but as one who has struggled with feeling like the kid who is never invited to the party, I understand how others can feel that way too. I also know that life is better outside the silo when we reconnect with others in a meaningful way. The bridges we need have already been built. We just need to cross over. It's a journey I invite you to take with me in the pages that follow.

How Can a Reality Star Be Our Guide?

I know what you have to be thinking right now. *What on earth does a former Bachelor have to say that could possibly matter?* You may not be thinking this, but believe me, I've asked myself this very question many times over the past year as I've worked on this book. It would be a lot easier for me to write a Bachelor "tell-all," but I couldn't bring myself to do that for my first book. Your time is too valuable for that, and so is mine. I wanted to write something that matters, and nothing matters more to me than addressing a yearning I've felt in my soul my entire life.

Over the past year this book has gone from being a vague idea to a cry from my spirit for the lonely and the isolated. I want to speak to those of us who feel a bit lost, who struggle with life's disappointments and unanswerable questions. Rather than offer platitudes and clichés, I invite you to explore the dark questions with me in the hope that together we can discover the light. Others have blazed a trail before us, which is why much of what follows is devoted to stories of those who have lived in these dark places and discovered hope in the midst of them. At times I share parts of my story, but I do so to encourage you to think through your own story.

Maya Angelou once said that there is no greater agony than bearing an untold story. For much of my life, I told myself a story that wasn't entirely true. I pray that in the pages that follow, we can each discover the true story of us, stories that will connect rather than isolate us further from one another. I want this book to be a safe place for you to explore the dark moments of your own story with the assurance that you are not alone in this journey. We're doing this together.

But I still haven't answered the question of why I am qualified to be the one to guide us on this journey. To be honest with you, I don't have an answer to that. I'm not a relationship expert, if such a thing even exists. I've laughed many times at the thought that because I went on reality television, my words now somehow matter. The truth is, I've always had something to say, but for twenty-five years my friends, family, and the occasional unfortunate person sitting next to me on a plane were the only ones to hear it. Now, for reasons I don't understand, my life has become very visible, and that's given me a platform I do not take lightly.

The journey I invite you to take with me is one I started long before I first stepped in front of the television cameras. What we are about to walk through together is a love letter to all of us. I promise these pages are soaked with tears, fears, frustrations, and joy. They are sacred to me. I hope they will be to you. Our shared feelings of loneliness and isolation are what bring us together for this trip, but that's only the starting point. The cure for isolation is connection, not just with others and romantic partners—although that is a given—but with God and even with ourselves. I have discovered that all four are interconnected. For me, the first step of this journey begins with a question many of us struggle to answer: Who are you?

PART I

———

NO LONGER ALONE

Reconnected to Myself

CHAPTER 1

Who Are You?

One of my favorite stories in the Bible is the woman at the well. The story goes like this: Jesus and his disciples had been walking all day. They were tired and thirsty and far from home when they came upon a well. Not that the well did them a lot of good, since they didn't have anything to draw water with. But it did give them a place to sit and rest, which is what they did until the sounds of rumbling stomachs convinced Jesus' disciples to go into town to find some food for their group.

But finding food wasn't going to be their biggest problem. They had ventured outside of Judea into Samaria, and the Jews and Samaritans didn't get along even a little bit. The two had a lot of bad blood that went back seven hundred years. On top of that the Samaritans didn't follow the dietary laws that made food kosher for the Jews. But the disciples were hungry enough that they went off looking for something to eat anyway.

Jesus didn't go with them; he sat down at the well and waited. Reading the story, I don't think he was there for the water.

Eventually a Samaritan woman came along to draw water. She nearly fell over when Jesus asked her for a drink. It wasn't just the bad blood between Jews and Samaritans that gave her pause. She was a woman, and in the first century, men in that part of the world didn't talk to women in public, not even their own wives. Jesus broke that taboo.

But she wasn't just a woman. She was a woman with a reputation, the kind of reputation that made her an outcast even among her own people. That's probably why she came to the well alone. Back in that day, women usually traveled in groups when they went outside of town to draw water. A woman traveling alone put herself at great risk of being attacked. But this woman came alone, most likely because the other women didn't want to associate with her due to her reputation and the decisions she had made. She didn't realize it yet, but Jesus didn't care about her reputation or how she'd attained it. Nothing she could say could shock him into walking away from this divine appointment.

What grabs my attention about this story, which you can find in John 4 in the Bible, is not the fact that Jesus talked to this woman, but how he talked to her. He spoke to her human to human, looking across at her, not down. Jesus' words held no judgment, no condemnation, which was a whole new experience for her.

She was so used to people putting her down, pointing out all her past mistakes, that she had trouble carrying on a real conversation with Jesus without immediately defending herself and jumping behind labels. "You are a Jew and I am a Samaritan," she immediately said when Jesus asked her for a drink. "How can you ask me for a drink?"

Jesus didn't come all this way to debate the ancient problems between these two people groups. He didn't care about the labels people used to divide themselves. No, he cared about her, and I think she could sense that. Instead of letting himself get pulled into her label game, Jesus offered her something she probably thought was out of her reach. He offered her a fresh start. But before he could get her to see the gift from God that was hers for the taking, he needed her to open her eyes to see something she'd never seen before: herself. Through their conversation Jesus kept probing, trying to get her to understand that she had no idea who she really was.

The woman at the well isn't the only one who struggles with understanding her identity. I think most people do. I know I do.

One of These Things

When I was little, I watched a lot of *Sesame Street*. One of my favorite skits was Ernie singing the legendary, brilliant song that began with the line, "One of these things is not like the others." I can't count the number of times I sang along with Ernie as he danced and sang in front of three red firefighter helmets and one silver hat or three sandwiches and a mitten. Right off I knew the one thing that didn't belong. Sure, it wasn't the toughest test in the world, but then again, I was only four.

Even after I outgrew *Sesame Street*, the "One of These Things" song stuck in my head because it gave me a label that told me who I was: the odd one out. The outsider. It wasn't the last label I affixed to myself. Most of my life I've mistakenly believed that sticking a label on my forehead somehow tells the truth about who I really am. Through most of school I was an athlete. If someone wanted to know who I was, the answer was easy: I was a jock. Until I wasn't. My athletic career ended with high school. I could forever live in the false reality of my high school years and think of myself as a great quarterback who can still throw a football a mile, but that's not true. Even when I started for my high school football team, "jock" was something I did. It wasn't who I was.

After college I spent a year in Peru teaching English as a second language. I guess that made me a teacher, although, since I didn't major in education, I never really thought of myself that way. Nor did I see teaching as a possible career path. Going to Peru was more about helping others and maybe finding myself. I accomplished one of the two, I think.

After Peru I moved to Denver and took a job writing software manuals. Technically that made me a writer, but I didn't feel like one. Even as I write this book, I'm not sure I feel like one. A few years later, I went on a reality dating show. Every time the network showed me on television, they added an identifying attribution: Ben H., Software Salesman. I guess they did that because it took up less space than "writes software manuals no one will ever read," but it still didn't answer the question of who I am.

After my time on two shows, I went through a stage where I was the "single friend," the one unattached guy whom all of my friends, and a lot of my mom's friends, tried to set up with the perfect girl. I got a lot of extra attention as the single friend, so much that it started to become a part of my identity. But it still wasn't who I really was or am, especially since I'm no longer single.

And that's the problem I run into whenever I slow down enough to ask myself who I am. Every time I stumble upon a label that I think might identify me, it eventually gets stripped away. The truth of who we are goes deeper than any label that has been placed on us or that we can give ourselves, but that doesn't stop us from hiding behind disposable layers. Even today, when I meet people for the first time and they want to know more about me, I usually say something like, "I'm Ben, and I run a for-purpose coffee company called Generous that creates sustainable jobs globally while also connecting people over a cup of coffee." In short, what I am saying is, "I'm Ben, and I have a job"—nothing more. You might be able to connect the dots and figure out that I like coffee and have a deep desire to make a difference in people's lives, but I still haven't told you who I am. Maybe that's because I struggle with figuring that out myself.

The same would be true if I asked who you are, and you described what you do. "I'm a doctor. I'm a lawyer. I'm a barista. I'm a mom. I'm a single dad. I work two jobs while paying off my student loans. I watch a lot of television. I am busy." None of these descriptors tell me who you are, and yet these are the answers we give when someone asks about us. *Who are you?* we hear, and we immediately start going through a list of jobs and responsibilities we try to hold together. Why?

Maybe that's why I've struggled with feeling like an outsider. How can I fit in when I don't even know who I am? I am not a label, and I am not the degree I received in my few years of school! How can any of us know who we are if we define ourselves by the labels that have been placed on us? Yet that takes us right back to the question that's so hard to answer: Who am I?

The Stories We Tell Ourselves

I grew up in one of the first generations that was consistently told we were special, that we could do anything we set our minds to. Be the first person to step foot on Mars? Of course that can be you, we were told. Pitch in the major leagues? Even though the odds of becoming a professional athlete are astronomically small, why not? You're special enough to do it, adults assured us. Become the next great singing star? What can stop you? A little thing like having no musical talent shouldn't get in the way of your dream. Do you want to be president? All you have to do is believe in yourself and you can do it, well-meaning adults said with a smile. "If you can believe it, you can achieve it," my generation was told over and over and over again.

Except my parents never told me that. I always wondered why. When I watched television, I heard the TV moms and dads build their kids up while a piano played softly in the background. The super-encouraging mom or dad talk was pretty much a staple of shows geared for kids back in the nineties. Some days I even got mad at my mom and dad because they didn't encourage me to do the impossible. They came to my basketball games where I was a standout player, but afterward I never heard them boasting to their friends about how I was going to play in the NBA someday. It's not that they told me I sucked at sports, nor did they hint that my drawing of a horsey and a ducky wasn't good enough to be placed on the refrigerator. They hung plenty of my drawings around the house, but they never told me I had the potential to be the next Rembrandt. They were too realistic for that.

As I got a little older, I got over being mad at my parents for not telling me I could do anything I set my mind to. I came to the realization that they were actually doing me a favor. I wasn't cut out to be a doctor or an astronaut. Even if I wanted to run for political office, the odds of me ever becoming president are around a trillion to one. I'm glad they never built me up and made me believe that I was destined to star in the NBA or find a cure for cancer. Thanks to my parents' real-ism, I never once thought my self-worth as a person lay in achieving some huge goal. They also did not instill in me the belief that my future happiness lay in becoming what eight-year-old Ben said he wanted to be when he grew up.

Don't get me wrong, I believe in the power of dreams. Everyone needs goals, especially goals pursued with a level of healthiness. We need targets to aim for or we'll never hit anything. Yet our dreams exist for us; we don't exist for them. Unfortunately, I've seen the opposite happening to my generation.

The dreams of what we wanted to be when we grew up turned into the stories we used to define ourselves. Who are you? I'm the future doctor. I'm the future baseball star. I'm the future leader of the free world. And when these dreams do not come true, it is devastating. We feel like we've let everyone down: our parents and grandparents, who sacrificed so much to help us reach for the stars; our teachers, who believed in us and encouraged us; and especially ourselves. When the dreams our eight-year-old selves staked out become our identity, and then those dreams do not come true, *loser* and *failure* become our new identity. It can be even worse when the dreams do come true, but they're not accompanied by a healthy balance of humility and grati-tude. Even with that balance, though, achieving our lifelong goals often leads to disappointment when we discover that reaching the stars does not automatically translate into a happier, more fulfilling life.

Most of the people I meet are somewhere in between. The stories we told ourselves of who we were going to be someday haven't yet come true, and maybe they never will, but we keep holding out hope that our happy ending is just around the corner. The hardest truth we will ever tell ourselves is *who I am now is who I am always going to be*. While I believe it is important to pursue goals and dreams in life, I must always remember that when my goals become my identity, I live in a constant disconnect between my dreams and reality. "Who are you?" we hear, and the answer is, "I'm going to be an X, Y, or Z." But who are you if X, Y, or Z never comes true? X, Y, or Z are just labels. So who are you when all the labels are stripped away?

Stripping Away the Chaos

Jesus never actually asked the woman at the well who she was, but she told him anyway. "I'm a Samaritan," she said, but Jesus didn't care. *Jew, Samaritan, Gentile, or any other label you want to throw at me. None of them matter,* Jesus essentially said. *I have the gift of living water, the gift that will wash away your past failures and disappointment and bring refreshment to your soul. It's yours if you want it.* She still didn't get it. She threw out more labels she'd always used to identify herself. She was a relationship failure and a religious outsider. *That's who I am*, she practically screamed. Jesus didn't buy it.

None of the woman at the well's labels defined her any more than all the labels we affix to ourselves. Yet we keep clinging to them like a "Hello, my name is" sticker worn at work conferences. And that's what disconnects us from ourselves and from other people. We work hard to convince ourselves that our identity can be captured by a label or by our accomplishments or by the stories we tell ourselves of all we're going to do someday, and yet we know none of these stories are enough. Deep down we know we have to be more.

Now this is the point in the chapter where I'm supposed to tell you how to go about discovering your true self. I'm sorry, but I can't do that. I struggle with doing that myself. I can, however, tell you where we all need to start. Before we can answer the question, "Who am I?" we must first break down the facades and excuses and the shame and the guilt and the pride and everything else we use to define ourselves. All the labels must be thrown out. Only once everything else has been stripped away can we know who we are.

I can't tell you who you are. That's not my job. And it's not your parents' job or your significant other's job or your boss's job or your pastor's job or anyone else's job. Only you can know who you are right now. And the question is not who you were in high school or who you will be if you land that dream job or finally find your soul mate. The question is, *Who are you right now, in this moment?* Until you can answer that question honestly, you cannot start on this journey of reconnecting with yourself or anyone else. Stripping everything away is frightening. It leaves us naked and afraid. But let me reassure you: you are not alone. We are all in the same position.

I realize I've just given you what feels like an impossible task, but here's where I've found help pursuing the answer. When I look inside myself, I can't always see the truth. Maybe I never can. Either I'm too full of myself because life is going great, or I'm too down on myself because I'm in a bad place. What I need is an outside, objective view of myself from someone who sees past all the covers I hide behind, and God himself is the only one I've found who can do that. Turning to God brings us back to the woman at the well.

Jesus didn't see her failures or her labels. He saw her in a way she'd never seen herself, and he opened up her eyes to see the same thing.

Her moment of self-discovery is beautiful. Go and read the story for yourself. You witness all of her shame from her past melting away. Instead of hiding, she runs back to the town that shunned her, unashamed and unafraid. "Come and see the One we've been waiting for!" she called out. She didn't try to keep Jesus to herself. Once she saw herself the way Jesus saw her, it changed the way she saw everyone else. Reading that story makes me wish that we all could have the same epiphany. I long for the day when we see ourselves the way God sees us and we draw our identity from him. If we ever do, it will also change the way we see everyone else. We'll not only peel off all the labels we stuck on ourselves, we will stop putting labels on others as well.

The Bible is filled with imagery that shows us how God sees us. One of my favorites is where he is the potter and I am the clay in his hands. When I look at myself through this lens, I see the One who loves me more than I can imagine taking his time to shape me into something beautiful. He uses every choice I make and every experience I go through in life to form me into someone who is ideally becoming more and more like him.

I've not done a lot of work with clay, but I know the potter's hands always get messy. I don't think God minds. He's willing to muddy himself as he shapes me. This picture also tells me that nothing I go through is ever wasted. I'm not the same person I was five years ago, or even five months ago. In the hands of the Potter, I'm constantly changing, and that's a good thing.

This is where we find the answer to our question, *Who am I?* I am a work in progress in the hands of the One who loves me. I have value and purpose and a reason for existing, not because of what I have done or what I will do, but because this is how God has made me and sees me. When everything else has been stripped away—all the guilt, shame, and disappointment—I stand naked before God, and in his eyes I am beautiful and beloved.

This is who I am, and it is enough.

CHAPTER 2

But a Breath

A direct message from someone named Caroline popped up on my Instagram account one day.

> Hey Ben, you don't know me, but I have a really good friend,
> Annie, who is losing her battle with CF. I'm reaching out to people
> Annie admires and asking them if they'd post a short video to
> encourage her on her Instagram page. Thanks.

After visiting Annie's Instagram page to make sure the request was legit, I told Caroline I'd be happy to help. I shot a quick video on my phone and tagged Annie's page for her to see.

That well could have been the end of the story, but I could not stop thinking about Annie. From what I learned, she'd lived with cystic fibrosis her entire life, but she never let her sickness hold her back.

I discovered that she and her family had raised more than two million dollars for the Cystic Fibrosis Foundation, which is an incredible amount. In 2017, at the age of twenty, Annie had a double-lung transplant, then immediately had to have a second because of complications with the first. I watched a video she'd posted about her first year with her new lungs. When she shot the video, she thought she'd turned a corner and could now live a normal life, but something went wrong. The disease came back. Yet, no matter what she'd been through, she remained a beautiful, vibrant, hope-filled young woman who made the most of every moment of every day.

The more I thought about Annie, the more my heart ached. By coincidence or God's providence, I happened to be back home in Indiana when Caroline first contacted me. Something about being back home, in the house where I grew up, made Annie's story hit me even harder.

My parents' house is the place I spent my days as a boy, completely free of all worries and fears and responsibilities. Even now, when I go back, I feel all the stresses of life melt away. My parents live on a lake, which is my refuge, my place to rest and unwind and recharge. On this particular visit, though, sitting outside with them on their deck, looking out at the water on one of those summer days that makes me love visiting Indiana, everything looked different. Even though my parents taught me never to take this life for granted, I did. All my life I'd taken this place, this lake, and my mom and dad living here for granted, like these gifts had always been here for me and always would be. Until I read Caroline's message. Now I couldn't think about anything except this twenty-two-year-old girl who didn't know if she had days or weeks or only hours left on this earth. Over the next few days I prayed for

Annie, just as I promised her I would in the video message I sent, but I felt like I needed to do more.

After my video posted, Caroline texted me.

> Hi Ben! I wanted to tell you Annie (your fan losing her battle to CF; she has had 2 dbl lung transplants & needs a 3rd but is too sick) got your video & it made her SO happy. You're so thoughtful & really made her feel so special . . . your kind words touched her & her family!! I went to visit with her 3 days last week & while she won't get better (her lungs are failing & nothing docs can do . . . there have only been 11 successful third dbl lung transplants & Annie is just too sick/it's too risky), she is in great spirits (pic attached!!).

I sat and stared at Annie's photo. *Two double-lung transplants and she needs a third but that can't happen, and my little thirty-second video made her SO happy? How? I can't just leave it at that,* I thought. I watched a video Annie and her friends had posted. She was so full of life even though she was so close to the end of hers. Her video had blown up across the internet, moving everyone who watched it. I could hardly hold myself together. *This girl . . . Wow, this girl.*

I texted Caroline back.

> Thanks for the update. I'm glad my little video touched her.

I paused for a moment and thought about what I should write next.

> Would it be possible for me to get Annie's number? I'd like to reach out to her.

Then I hit SEND.

My phone dinged almost immediately.

Sure. Her number is _____.

I clicked the number and typed,

Hi Annie, this is Ben Higgins. Caroline gave me your number. I hope it's okay for me to text you.

Annie texted right back. I didn't save her first text, but I did save many of those that followed. I can't bring myself to delete them. They feel . . . sacred.

I told Annie how she had inspired me. She replied,

Yeah, I'm trying to turn this into something positive. I always wanted to make an impact on this world, and now I'm finally getting the chance. I always wanted to get into YouTube or something, but I was afraid of being judged/didn't know if anyone would want to hear what I had to say. It was my dream job, because I can't have a regular job since my immune system is so suppressed. I was sad at first thinking finally I can do my dream job, like maybe I have the platform & it kinda broke my heart thinking that all my dreams are coming true when my life is coming to an end. It didn't seem fair. But I'm not going to think like that. Instead I'm using it to push me to get better and better so that I can live out my dreams for as long as I can.

We texted back and forth for a while that day and some the next and the next until talking with her was like talking to any of my other friends. She kept asking about me, but I wanted to know about her. Her attitude in the face of death just blew me away. Even though Annie was only twenty-two, she seemed to have a much better grasp on life than nearly anyone I'd ever met. And that's what I really wanted to ask her about.

I texted her one day:

You spoke about wanting to help people recognize the fragility of life. In your twenty-two years, what have you learned about life? What do you tell people?

She replied,

I have definitely learned a lot, and I've spoken at many events about many different things such as organ donation, finding a cure for CF, motivational speaking. But one thing that I've always said was that I never let CF define me. I never kept it hidden, but it was just a part of me. I always made my messages about how I was a fighter and I would never give up. If I gave in, then I would be letting CF win and take over. I knew I was going to die earlier than most, and I always said that as long as we cherish every moment and take the time to live life, our lives would be worth it.

I wept as I read those words. *"I knew I was going to die earlier than most, and I always said that as long as we cherish every moment and take the time to live life, our lives would be worth it."*

I had just turned thirty, which is one of those birthdays where people act like you're old, but you aren't. Before I met Annie, I felt like I had all the time in the world in front of me, but reading her texts, I tried to see the world through her eyes. Life is so short. It just keeps pushing you along like one of those moving walkways in the airport. We jump on and move forward while life moves past us. We watch it go by, but we are moving too quickly to grasp anything until we hit the very end. And by then it is too late. Annie's life was shorter than most, but life for everyone is but a breath. I'd always known this, but up until that moment I'd done nothing to get out in front of it or prepare for it.

That doesn't mean I'd never thought about death. I have moments where I lie in bed and my mind starts wandering and a darkness sweeps over me. I ask myself, *What if . . . ? The only thing I've ever known is breath. There's sun and there are family and faith and love and friends and celebration and laughter and tears and life. What if it were all taken away? If is not the right word, because it will all be taken away someday. The only question is when.*

Can I be honest with you? Thinking about my own mortality and how fragile life really is scares me. Just to think that everything I've ever known, everything I take for granted, everything I've loved, all of it will be gone in the blink of an eye as this life comes to an end. I am but a breath, and so are you.

And here was this beautiful young woman telling me to cherish every moment. I texted back to her,

What is something you would tell someone who is young and
healthy to look for in life?

Her reply was the second half of her last text. I'm going to include all of it because she nails exactly what I want this chapter to say:

Then when I needed to go to the 3rd transplant I knew I had to fight again. And I was super tired, as the last 3 years were wild in terms of all the crazy health things that went on. The doctors all told me that if I didn't want to go for a 3rd, no one would judge me, because no one knows if it will even work since there have been 11 in the US and 3 at Duke (where I was going) but I told them, nope, I'm going to fight. I told them if I just get one week being able to breathe again, it would be worth all the pain and torture. And then I was told it was over. And there was nothing more they could do. I was scared and frustrated and felt like I was disappointing everyone. I didn't just fight by myself. I had friends, families, doctors. I had my army behind me fighting too. I wanted to continue to fight for them and for myself! When that video was taken that went viral* I was so out of it. I was told I had 48 hours to live, and so my friends wanted to cheer me up. I was so happy and so grateful that all these people were reaching out to me, but part of it made me sad because, yeah, I would love to meet Taylor Swift, but the way it was happening was because I was dying. I saw news articles saying "gravely sick girl's final wish was to meet Taylor Swift." That's not me. *Yes, I had only 2 weeks to live, but I'm so much more than just a sick girl* (emphasis added). My friends and family all explained to me that they just need clickbait, and that everyone would see that I've fought my

---

* Annie's friends posted a video of Annie and her friends singing and dancing to Taylor Swift's "Shake It Off," which went viral. When Taylor Swift learned of it, she did a FaceTime call with Annie.

whole life speaking about life and how fragile it is, so we have to cherish everything in the moment and just be happy. I wanted the world to hear my voice, because this is such an important message, as simple as it is.

No one will ever fully be ready for death. We don't know when it's coming. So we have to live while we have the chance, because when that chance is taken away is when you will want it the most. Every time I get a video or message or comment with people saying kind things, it's so inspiring to me. That people understand what I'm trying to say is truly incredible. Also, we haven't stopped all medicine. I just also have medicine to keep me comfortable. Normally you can only have one or the other, but the doctors at Columbia found a way to make it so that I can have both. We are hoping to potentially stabilize me and live as long as possible. We really have no idea how much longer I have, but I'm taking it day by day because all the doctors have been shocked at how I bounce up and down health-wise. They don't think I have a lot of time, but they do think I have more fight in me. So our plan is to have fun, stay comfortable, and live life to the fullest. Hopefully check off bucket list items and show the world how important it is to live even [when] it's coming to the end. I would tell them just to enjoy life. I have healthy teenage sisters & they get caught up in things that in the grand scheme of life don't matter too much. This too shall pass. Now that I do have this ticking clock, my sisters are cherishing the moments we have together too. I have a video camera that I am going to make videos explaining my whole health story, maybe give tips and tricks to other chronically ill patients, some beauty videos because that's always been a dream of mine, but mostly videotaping my days and all the bucket list items I want to do to show and inspire that dying doesn't have to be scary . . . it can be beautiful!! and then my sisters/friends/family/whoever else will have that forever.

If you and I were sitting next to one another talking, there'd be a long silence right here. I'm just . . . I'm blown away by Annie's words. She said so much in this one text. Reread her message. First, she wrote, "Yes, I had only two weeks to live, but I'm so much more than just a sick girl." I'm going to come back to this idea in a later chapter, but for now, pay attention to what she is saying. This section of the book is all about reconnecting with yourself. Here's a good first step: realize you are more than whatever it is you're struggling with.

"I'm so much more than just a sick girl," she said. Annie had battled CF her entire life, but she refused to let the disease define her. We all struggle with something, but Annie taught me I cannot let my struggles define me. I'm more than my problem. You are too.

The second part of her message will stick with me the rest of my life. She wrote, "No one will ever fully be ready for death. We don't know when it's coming. So we have to live while we have the chance, because when that chance is taken away is when you will want it the most." This is one of the most profound statements I've ever heard. Live while you have the chance, because that chance will be taken away someday. Life is but a breath, and that breath will soon be taken away from us. The question we now face is one Annie answered beautifully: If life is short and a gift, how can we best use it?

In my experience, any answer to this question that makes me greater than and others less than is a bad answer. When our lives are focused only on ourselves, we are further disconnected from ourselves by settling for the smallest answer possible regarding what we want out of life.

The third lesson is one Annie had for her sisters, but it applies to everyone: "I have healthy teenage sisters, and they get caught up in things that in the grand scheme of life don't matter too much. This too shall pass." Life is short. Why do we waste it on things that don't matter? I think that's one of the reasons for the great disconnect so many of us feel. We spend so much time on things that really don't mean anything that we have little time or energy left for the things that do. Annie taught me to turn that around.

And then her final words in her message: "Dying doesn't have to be scary . . . it can be beautiful!" Annie and I talked on the phone about that one. She explained to me she wasn't afraid of death because of what was on the horizon. Her attitude wasn't, "Hey, I hope I get to heaven one day," hoping for the best, but a settled confidence that came out of her faith in God. I have to tell you, her faith was different from what I usually come across. Hers was not some sort of transactional commitment that says, "If I accept you, God, and follow you, then will you let me into heaven?" Instead, she had a settled faith. A faith where she understood she had purpose and value before God, and that purpose was to bring his light to this world through faith, hope, and love. She also knew that the role she'd played on this earth would not end once she died but would keep on growing and expanding.

I guess what I am trying to say is she lived with purpose, and that purpose allowed her to come face to face with death and make that encounter beautiful. If dying can be beautiful, how much more so can life?! That's the place I want each one of us to get to. It's not just about learning how to make the most of each moment we have on this earth, but making those moments a thing of joy and beauty. I've met a lot of people who simply endure life as if every breath is a punishment. Annie enjoyed every second she had. For her, every breath was a gift from God to be savored. That's how I want to live.

Annie only had twenty-two years, but her life will be felt for a very long time. I pray the same can be said of me when my time on this earth comes to an end.

CHAPTER 3

Victim or Victor?

Pity is addictive, at least it is for me. Maybe that's why I find it so easy to embrace being an outsider. Every time I verbalize my feelings of pity, I'm usually met with a chorus of voices that say, "Oh, Ben, we didn't mean to leave you out. Why do you feel that way? Ben, you matter. Ben, you are important. Ben, we get you. Ben, you'll find someone who will love you. Oh, poor, poor Ben. You don't deserve any of this."

As much as I hate to admit it, the chorus of "poor, poor Ben" resonates with something deep inside me, even as I keep looking for a way to deny it does. I think it resonates with all of us. When other people express pity for us, we often find a measure of comfort in it. Their words validate our feelings—and sometimes they are legitimate feelings—but it tips over into being less than healthy when they also reassure us that we're the victim here and someone else is to blame for how bad we feel about ourselves. Their pity lulls us into feeling free not to take ownership of our circumstances. After all, someone else did us wrong. Our situation isn't our fault. Who, then, can blame us for lying here in our pain, unable to move forward with life? We've been wronged. We need people's pity. We need the sympathy.

This victim mindset becomes our get-out-of-jail-free card. We can lash out at other people because no one will call us out on it. How can they? We're only acting out because of what we've been through. All their objections to our bad behavior can be swept away by telling them they'd do the same if they'd been through what we've been through.

I can easily fall into this trap. That is, until I meet someone like Brandon.

Brandon's Story

Brandon always wanted to make a difference in people's lives. That's what attracted him to my coffee company. It wasn't so much our coffee that brought him into my life but his desire to connect with people and, maybe, in the process, make life better for others. That was my partner's and my goal when we created Generous and its ambassador program.

Generous Ambassadors are less ambassadors for our coffee than for our mission; they are men and women who communicate and advocate on behalf of Generous to the public. The tasks of the Ambassadors are to voluntarily commit their time and resources to selling products, setting up fundraisers, and enhancing brand reputation. They do this because they believe that through the ambassador program more generosity, kinship, and kindness can be shared. We started the program to give people an entry point to do good and to serve others. Long before he ever heard of me or Generous, Brandon was already on board with the idea of making the world a better place through serving others. When he found out about our ambassador program, it felt like a perfect fit. Signing up didn't mark some dramatic change in his life. For Brandon, becoming a Generous Ambassador was just one more step in a lifetime of serving, although this was his first new service venture since a skiing accident the previous winter had left him paralyzed at a point halfway between his ribs and belly button.

Finding a new outlet to serve others so soon after completing his rehab from a life-changing injury might seem unusual, and I guess maybe it is. But it didn't seem that way to Brandon. Serving others is who he is. At the age of twenty-five, life threw him one of the most radical disconnects any person can experience. In the blink of an eye, he went from being a six-foot-one former college baseball player, who still competed daily in any way he could, to a wheelchair-bound paraplegic. Brandon moved to Denver for the mountain sports, only to lose the use of his legs during his first Colorado ski trip.

I think most people would call that turn of events unfair, and they'd be right. If anyone deserves pity and a flood of sympathy, it's Brandon. One look at his chair and you almost feel obligated to feel sorry for him, but to Brandon, pity is an insult. He's never seen himself as a victim, and he doesn't want you to either.

Brandon doesn't remember his accident. One second he was skiing down a mountain, and the next he was looking up from a hospital bed as a doctor told him he'd never walk again. Earlier that day, he and his girlfriend and a group of their friends had driven to Breckenridge for a day of skiing. Even though his friends were experienced skiers, they all stuck close to Brandon on the beginner, or green circle, slopes. A natural athlete, Brandon got the hang of skiing pretty quickly. By the afternoon he was ready to join his friends on the blue square, or intermediate, slopes. With every run down the blue slopes, he became more and more comfortable on his skis until he felt like he'd been doing this all his life. Toward the end of the day, his group decided to take one last run down one of the blue slopes, which would take them closer to their car. Brandon never made it down the hill.

The last run of the day started out like all the rest. Brandon fell a little behind the rest of his group, but he motioned them to keep going. He'd catch up with them at the bottom of the hill. By this point in the day, no one felt like they needed to hang back with Brandon since he could ski nearly as well as the rest of his group.

He could have gone faster down the hill, but he was careful to keep cutting back and forth to control his speed. Although he felt confident, he also knew his limitations. He told himself there was no sense taking any unnecessary chances. With each cut his skis dug into the snow, but once or twice they bounced instead. The bounces got his attention.

The sun sank lower in the sky, and the powder had started turning into ice. The farther down the hill Brandon went, the icier it became and the less his skis dug in when he tried to cut. His speed started to build until he found himself going faster than he had all day. Up ahead the run split left and right, with a large signpost displaying arrows showing where to turn. Brandon tried to cut to the right before he reached the sign, but he was going too fast and the run was too icy. So instead of turning, he slammed headfirst into the post.

Witnesses later wondered how Brandon survived the crash. He probably would not have if not for a retired doctor, a hand surgeon, who was coming down the hill right behind him. The doctor called the ski patrol, who radioed for a Flight for Life helicopter. In the meantime, Brandon was spitting up blood and complaining he couldn't feel his legs. The Flight for Life helicopter arrived within minutes. Paramedics secured him to a backboard, loaded him in the helicopter, and transported him to Saint Anthony Hospital in Lakewood, just outside of Denver. There, doctors discovered Brandon had severe internal bleeding due to a nick in his aorta. In addition, he had five broken ribs, lung damage, and had shattered his spine at the T9 vertebra. They rushed him into emergency surgery to stop the internal bleeding. Later, Brandon was told he'd lost three liters of blood. Most people do not survive losing two. The next day brought more surgery as doctors fused his spine back together from the T6 to the T11. It was around this time he woke up to hear the doctor tell him he'd never walk again.

Brandon's parents immediately flew from Wisconsin to be by his side. His girlfriend stayed with him around the clock as well. She also just happened to be a nurse at the children's hospital. Since Brandon had no experience with hospitals or medical terminology, every time doctors came in to talk to him about his injuries and prognosis, she translated for him. He'd look at her and ask, "Okay, what does that mean for me?" And what it meant looked really bad, at least in terms of ever getting his old life back.

Thankfully, the people he loved made it clear that nothing had changed for them. His girlfriend reassured him that she still saw him as the same man he was before the accident. "Whether you can walk or run or even stand again doesn't matter to me," she told him multiple times. Other people with similar injuries whom Brandon met during his recovery weren't so lucky. One of the guys he met during his rehabilitation opened up and told Brandon how he was engaged before he was injured. The paralysis turned out to be too much for the relationship. The guy's fiancée called off the wedding and left him alone. Hearing that story made Brandon appreciate his girlfriend's commitment even more.

Brandon spent three weeks in the intensive care unit, during which he had to have another surgery to repair a leaking duct. The day after Christmas doctors transferred him to a rehab hospital in Englewood, Colorado. When he first entered the rehabilitation hospital, Brandon's doctors told him he'd be there a minimum of eight weeks. Even eight weeks seemed like hardly any time for someone who had to relearn how to do everything. From getting dressed to going to the bathroom to bathing to navigating his own kitchen, Brandon had to relearn every life skill. Through it all he had one goal: independence. That was the goal of his physical therapists as well. Although Brandon knew he could never regain his old life, everyone he worked with wanted to help him attain something as close to it as possible.

Brandon was an eager student. He approached his rehab with the same intensity he had when he played college baseball. Every day he wanted to get better than the day before, while his friends and family and the hospital staff surrounding him cheered him on. He connected with other patients who got released but came back as outpatients. Seeing their progress spurred him on. Their experience showed him what was possible, and Brandon was determined to squeeze as much out of his body as he could.

All of Brandon's hard work paid off when, after only six weeks, his doctors told him he could go home. He still had a lot of work to do, but at least now he could do it as an outpatient. Just over two months after his accident, his girlfriend drove him back to his apartment. He was home.

The moment he finally wheeled himself through his front door, reality hit him: *This is my life. My legs don't work, and there's absolutely nothing I can do about it. Ever.* It wasn't just being in his wheelchair in an old, familiar place that drove this truth home, but all the unfamiliar changes his family had made to his apartment while he was in the hospital. His kitchen was different. The upper cabinets had been emptied and the contents moved to the low shelves where he could reach them from his chair. Prior to his injury, Brandon was over six feet tall. Now he had the vertical reach of a child. Nothing in his bathroom felt familiar. Adaptive equipment had been installed for his shower, vanity, even on the toilet. He felt out of place in his bedroom, his living room, and everywhere he went. This was his home, but with all the changes it didn't feel like it. Instead of being able to relax and feel like himself again, he found himself surrounded by reminders of how different his life was always going to be. He didn't like it, but what could he do about it?

The Mindset of a Victor

The day Brandon came home to his apartment was the first of many dark days. Another came a few days later. He'd wheeled himself into the bathroom and took a long look at himself in the mirror for the first time. He pulled off his shirt and stared at the scar that started in the middle of his chest, dipped down under his right pec, and ran under his arm and around to his back. The scar came from the incision the doctors made in his first emergency surgery. Sitting there, staring at the scar, he began to wonder why. *Why did this happen to me? What did I ever do to deserve this?*

Before he fell into full-blown self-pity mode, another thought hit him. He took another look at the scar, but it looked different this time. Instead of telling him he was the victim of a horrible accident, he thought about the doctor who had found him on the slopes and the team at the hospital that had saved his life. Without the scar, he'd be dead. It wasn't a reminder of how life had treated him unfairly, it was a reassurance that—even on his worst day—God was watching out for him.

Brandon is a Christ follower. Before his accident he talked a lot about trusting God with all of his life, but the reality of what that looked like had never been so clear. If a doctor had not been right behind him, whoever did eventually find him wouldn't have known what to do to save his life. And even after making it to the hospital as quickly as he did, he should have bled out. He actually did bleed out but somehow survived, even though he lost more than half the blood in his body. *God was there. He protected me. He saved my life,* Brandon realized. Self-pity gave way to gratitude. Instead of being angry at what had happened to him and all he had lost, he became thankful for the gift of life he still had.

And that's the difference between being a victim or a victor. Victims hold on to the pain. They look around for someone to blame and crave the sympathy and pity of others. Their identity comes not just through whatever wrongs they've suffered, but from their status as victim. But when we choose the mindset of a victor, we choose to move forward in life no matter what the future may hold. Our stories move from being cries for pity to being a way to connect with others whom life has also hurt.

Some might look at Brandon and say he hasn't beaten his paralysis because he's still confined to a wheelchair and will be for the rest of his life. That misses the whole point. Life happens. Bad things hit everyone, some of which are so big and so life-altering that their effects stay with you the rest of your life, or even, as I discovered in Annie, cut your life short. Being a victor does not mean you have to "beat" paralysis or cancer or whatever it is you struggle with. It means choosing to go forward and treat every day as a gift from God.

A victor's mindset also requires you to become what Brandon called "an active participant in your own survival." He compared it to being stranded in the middle of the ocean. A victim just gives up and drowns. A victor treads water until help arrives, and when that help does arrive, a victor accepts it. Victors don't wave off the boats, telling rescuers they're going to swim across the ocean on their own. Victors do all they can to help themselves while also accepting help from those who care about them, and even seeking out that help when they need it. Victors aren't stubborn, and they aren't arrogant. The victor mindset comes down to having a positive outlook and opening your life up to other people, both to help them and to receive help from them. That's also called living in community, but that's for the next section of this book.

What Winning Looks Like

Brandon remembers the exact day he felt like he beat his injuries: June 8, 2019, six full months after his accident. He was in his car, driving home from a workout at a CrossFit gym not far from his house. He planned to go home, take a quick shower, then go grab a beer with a friend to catch up. Somewhere between the gym and his house it hit him: *I'm doing the exact same thing I would have done if I'd never hit that sign. I'd hit the gym, work out, then go hang out with my friends.* The only differences between his life then and now are the adaptive controls on his truck and how he uses a ramp instead of the stairs to go into the bar. Other than that, his life has not changed. As a former college baseball player, he knew all about curveballs, and life had just thrown him one. "You just have to adapt and react," he told me. That's what victors do.

I want you to go back and reread the last paragraph. By refusing to allow his limitations to define him, Brandon now lives free of resentment and anger. Instead of being stuck in an endless cycle of wallowing in self-pity, he's gotten on with his life. At first glance his story may seem very heavy, another in a long line of sad stories this Bachelor guy keeps piling on top of you. But it is not. When you see his wheelchair the way Brandon sees it, his life is wonderfully ordinary. He continues to live the life he always had, even though it looks different than it did before his one and only skiing trip.

A lot of us have gone through defining moments like Brandon's ski trip. While they may not be nearly as life-altering as his, these moments still mark life's sharp, painful turns. I don't know what you have been through that brings out the "poor, poor you" comments from friends and family, but let me tell you, pity may be addictive, but winning feels much, much better. Victim or victor, we get to choose which we will be.

CHAPTER 4

More Than Myself

I work very hard to find my identity in God's love and acceptance. Annie inspired me to make the most of every moment of every day, to realize I'm more than my struggles. Hanging out with Brandon pulls me out of my addiction to pity and moves me to adopt a victor's mindset. When I feel disconnected from myself, when I don't know who I am or why I am, when I struggle with feeling isolated and less than everyone else, these are the stories I go to as a way of reconnecting. All make me want to be the best version of myself.

But that's not always enough.

I say I want to be the best version of myself, but I have days when I do just the opposite. Some days I feel like what Paul described in Romans 7 where he wrote, "I want to do what is right, but I can't. I want to do what is good, but I don't. I don't want to do what is wrong, but I do it anyway" (vv. 18–19). I've had those days, but not just days.

As much as I hate to admit it, I've had long stretches of life where I wanted to do what was right, but it seemed I just couldn't pull it off. Even though I said I wanted to do what was good, I did the opposite. I said I didn't want to do what was wrong, then turned around and did it anyway.

I don't have to tell you how this all turned out, because I think all of us have fallen into this pit. Most people have periods of their lives where the way they live is completely disconnected from the way they say they want to live. When it happens it's hard not to end up pretty much hating ourselves for it. This is the worst kind of personal disconnect, and I've lived it. If we're completely honest, I think we all have. At least, all of my friends have.

When I find myself sucked down into this disconnect, no amount of Bible reading or inspirational stories can pull me out of it. Why? Because I completely lack perspective. All I can see is the worst in me. All I can feel is the guilt and shame and disgust over my own behavior. I get so down on myself that all I can see is down, down, down. I keep beating myself up like maybe I am trying to exact the punishment I think I deserve. I can see no other solution. I pull back from everyone, which only leaves me more stuck. I cannot, in that moment, reconnect with myself because I do not believe I am worth reconnecting with. In these moments I need help. I need a friend.

Holding Up a Mirror

For me, the hardest thing to do when I am disgusted with myself is to look in the mirror. The whole idea of coming face-to-face with myself throws me right back to whatever the incident was that made me so upset with myself. I don't even have to be upset to feel this way. As I expressed in the opening chapters, I have days when I feel very lonely and isolated, days when I feel like no one will ever get me or fully understand me. On those days, I don't have a problem with how other people see me but with how I see myself.

The reflection in the mirror is all wrong and distorted, like the fun house mirrors on the fifth floor of the Indianapolis Children's Museum. When you stand in front of one of these mirrors, you look super tall and skinny, and when you move to another, you look very short and fat. No matter where you look, you can never get a true reflection of yourself because the mirror won't allow it. What I need is a new mirror.

That's where a real friend comes in.

I cannot reconnect with myself on my own. I need a friend to come along and pull the fun house mirror out of my hand and hold up a true mirror that shows the real me. Even then, I have trouble seeing me, but a friend will not let me look away. "This is who you really are," they keep saying over and over until I finally get it.

When I feel worthless, a friend reminds me that I have value. When I feel isolated, a friend pulls me back in and tells me I matter. When I am overwhelmed with guilt over past mistakes, a friend reminds me that grace is available to give me a second chance. I've even had friends come to me with a mirror that showed the ugliness I needed to deal with when all I wanted to do was gaze in a magic mirror that told me how great I was. They told me I was wrong when no one else would. Those weren't easy words to hear. At first I fought back and tried to deny what they said, but my friends wouldn't put the mirror down until I saw the truth for myself. Man, those days were so hard but so necessary.

The only way any of us can fully reconnect with ourselves is to surround ourselves with friends who know us well enough and are brutally honest enough to never let us forget who we really are.

Getting Real

The hardest part of that last statement comes from the fact that, when we are disconnected from ourselves, we aren't sure who we are. Instead, we hide behind masks, projecting an image of what we hope to be—an image we want others to believe. And if that's true, then this has to be the most disconnected time in human history because masks form a major part of our culture.

Unconvinced? Stop reading for a moment and start scrolling through Instagram feeds. What do you see? You see everyone at their best. Their vacation pics show the dream vacation, the kind you know you'll never get to take. Their date photos show the perfect meal at the perfect restaurant with the perfect little touches like flowers and cards placed there by the perfect guy or gal. I know this is what people do because I do it! I don't post my disaster trips on Instagram or Twitter or Facebook. I don't post videos of me losing my cool with slow service at a restaurant or me getting angry because the airline lost my luggage. Maybe some people do, but I think most of us only show our best because that's the image we want to project. We only want others to see our best, even when our best is not who we are. And that's been true of human beings since long before social media was ever invented.

Most of the energy expended in relationships is spent trying to cover up the parts of ourselves we don't want anyone else to see. Everyone has something they want to hide, something ugly that would embarrass them if it got out. It's not that we're afraid of being embarrassed as much as we fear our so-called friends might cut and run if they saw the real us. Hiding our ugly requires an exhausting amount of energy. We end up expending so much energy trying to keep people from seeing who we really are that we can't even be sure who that is anymore, resulting in a giant disconnect within our souls. At some point we will all run out of gas, which is usually followed by a crisis and a crash.

It's not like this is anything new. That's been true of the human race since the beginning of time. The earliest glimpse of humanity can be found in the garden of Eden. In that story, the moment the ugly happened, the first two people covered up and hid and blame shifted. I think that's why we have an epidemic of surface-level friendships, where everyone pretends and hides and then, the moment things get hard, we run.

I thank God that the one thing that has most kept me connected to myself, the one thing that pulls me out from behind my masks, are the friends I have who know everything about me, who have seen the ugly and still accept me. They can tell when I'm pretending. They can tell when I'm not being honest with them and I'm not being honest with myself. But they don't leave me there, nor do they abandon me to my worst impulses. Instead, they come to me and tell me I don't have to hide the parts of my life I am embarrassed about. Without using words, they tell me they know that part of me scares me, but it doesn't scare them. More than that, they are willing to walk with me as I work through these ugly parts of myself. They pull me back into the light.

Everybody has dark days. Having friends who live in the light and know me better than I know myself keeps me from staying there. My friends know the dark is not where I want to be, and they help bring me home. I can't get there on my own. I gravitate toward the dark out of fear and embarrassment. My friends won't let me, because they know me better than that.

Borrowed Faith

One of my friends came to me the other day with a strange request. No one had ever asked me this question before. At first I didn't know what to say. He asked to borrow something, and of course I said yes. He's one of my closest friends. I'll give him anything even before he asks, but this request just seemed strange. I had no idea if he was serious. Maybe asking to borrow something I had no idea how to share gave him everything he needed. Before I tell you what he wanted, let me tell you a little more about my friend.

Two years ago this friend suffered a crisis of faith—not a crisis of faith in God or in himself, but in his life's work. Call it burnout or divine intervention, but for whatever reason my friend could no longer continue pouring himself into the work he'd been devoted to his entire adult life. His work wasn't just a job. It was a calling, a divine calling. For more than a decade and a half, he'd looked at his work as something good that improved the lives of those it touched. Over the past couple of years, however, doubt had crept in. The cause didn't look quite as noble as it once had. He'd always believed that if he did his job well, people would end up closer to God. After watching the results of his work and of those like him, he wondered if that was still true. With time he began to wonder if it had ever been true.

Finally, my friend had to leave his job. No one forced him out. He did that himself. He took an early retirement and walked out the door and into an uncertain future. My friend, like most guys, drew a great deal of his identity from his work. After he left his job, he realized it was more than he'd thought. Now he found himself in a vulnerable place emotionally and spiritually and, to a degree, financially. Some days were harder than others. Many days he got up in the morning, unsure of what he was going to do next but certain he'd made the right call by leaving his career. On those days he plotted out possible future paths and became very excited about what lay ahead. Those were the good days. But even though the good days far outnumbered the bad, the bad days made it difficult to get out of bed.

And that's why my friend had called me.

"Ben," he said, "I need to ask you for a favor."

"Sure," I said. "Anything."

Then he asked me the question no one had ever asked me before: "Can I borrow faith from you today?"

I agreed to lend him my faith and acted like I knew what he meant, but eventually I came clean. "How can I really help you today?" I asked.

"You know me," he said. "I need you to speak life over me. Rebuke me if I need it. Call me out if you see something in me that shouldn't be there. But, more than anything, I need some faith from you today because I don't have any, and I can't exist, much less thrive, without it."

Can I borrow faith from you today? is now one of my favorite requests. My friend didn't need to borrow faith in God from me, because my friend hadn't given up on God. No, what my friend really needed to hear was that God hadn't given up on him. Since God isn't in the habit of speaking in an audible voice to human beings, my friend needed to hear those words from me. He needed me to tell him not to quit, not to turn back, not to doubt the decision he'd reached after months, if not years, of soul-searching.

Giving him that faith was easy because over the years, he'd invested the same kind of faith in me. For years he had listened patiently when all I had were doubts. Never once did he judge me or act shocked when I allowed myself to become fully vulnerable before him. He also didn't push back when I put him in some uncomfortable situations, like the time I took him to Honduras on a mission trip and informed him when we arrived that he was supposed to speak to the crowd that had gathered to meet us. We hadn't even known one another that long when I did that to him. He didn't get mad at me over it—he trusted me and stood up before the crowd and spoke like he'd prepared his speech weeks in advance.

Over the years he'd invested a lot of trust in me, and now he needed to draw some back, like pulling money out of a savings account that has accrued interest over the long haul. My friend had become disconnected. He was searching, wondering who he was. He needed faith from me to help find his way back, and I gladly gave it.

Vulnerability and Grace

I kept trying to come up with the right word for how a friend helps you reconnect with yourself. *Love* works, since a real friend loves you even when you have trouble loving yourself. *Help* is a part of it. Friends help pick you up and hold you upright until your legs work for themselves. They don't run when things get ugly, and they sit with you through both your best and your worst days. They're there to celebrate the first and to help you survive the second. A friend sees the best in you when all you or anyone else can see is bad, and they also see the worst in you without believing the worst about you. Again, I kept trying to come up with a word to describe what a friend does as they help us reconnect with ourselves, but what word could possibly be big enough to encompass all of this, along with the thousands of parts of friendship I haven't mentioned?

And then it hit me.

A real friend is like Jesus in our lives. That made me think about how a friendship with Jesus is possible. And it is possible. Yet a friendship with Jesus is not something we earn by doing a lot of good stuff that impresses God. The Bible says there's only one thing that makes a friendship with Jesus possible and one thing that makes a relationship with God possible: grace. We can connect with God because of grace, and that's the same thing that makes friendships work. It all comes down to *grace.*

The Bible talks a lot about grace and how it opens the door to a real relationship with God. That's a topic I explore in depth in the last section of this book. A lot of us have trouble accepting the idea of grace from God because we experience so little of it in our own lives. It often feels like, as human beings, we find it much easier to spew cruelty instead of grace. If you have any doubt, read through the comments section of a public personality's social media posts. When a scandalous report comes out about someone who was once admired, there is no shortage of people who say, "Aha! Of course. I always knew there was something off about that guy." We believe the worst and we expect the worst of others, which may be why we have so much trouble when it comes to believing the best about ourselves as well. We need grace, and friends are there to extend it.

A true friend extends grace by accepting me where I am. They listen without being shocked and speak truth to me without judgment. A real friend sees through my excuses and gently confronts me with truth. It is easy to love me at my best, but real love and true relationships love me at my worst. That's the hardest and most necessary type of grace. A friend doesn't have to approve of what I've done to accept me as a person. Grace accepts without having to approve. Then real grace works to help me move past my failures and become the person I was created to be. Once again, I can't do this on my own because a friend gives grace when I need it the most, when I can't give it to myself.

Friends enable me to reconnect with myself. Therefore, to reconnect with myself, I have to connect with others. You cannot have one without the other, which is why we are just getting started on this journey together. I am convinced that we are better together, and I am better with you. But is that true? To find the answer I spent some time with a relatively new friend who spent most of his growing-up years completely cut off from others. Connecting beyond himself is a new experience for him, which is why I was eager to speak with him. I think we are better together, but would someone who lived most of his life isolated, not by choice but by the hand life dealt him, agree?

PART 2

NO LONGER ALONE

Reconnected to Others

CHAPTER 5

Better Together?

The question mark in this chapter title is not a typo. All my life I've heard how human beings are tribal and how our lives are better together. One of the first declarative statements by God in the Bible was, "It is not good for the man to be alone" (Genesis 2:18). Rick Warren, in his massive bestseller, *The Purpose Driven Life*, went so far as to call connecting with other people one of the five reasons why you and I are on this planet.[4] Without connections, without relationships, our lives will forever be aimless and empty, at least that's what I've always been taught.

But is that true?

Do we really need to connect in a meaningful way with other people for our lives to matter?

Are we really better together?

I know the Bible says that it's not good for a man to be alone, but

God made that statement about Adam before Eve, when the world population was at a grand total of one. A population of one will eventually become a population of zero. There's no danger of that happening now, so why do I need to connect with other people relationally?

If we're all completely honest, we have to admit that connecting with other people in meaningful relationships is not easy in part because such relationships demand a level of sacrifice and risk. Most people don't exactly stand in line to make selfless sacrifices that may or may not be appreciated and reciprocated. The human heart tends to default to selfishness, to wanting our own way. Why do we need relationships that challenge this desire?

And even if I can wrap my head around the idea that we need others, does that mean I need to move out beyond the relationships I'm already in? A lot of us have loving families. Isn't that enough? Who needs more? When I've been told that we need to have meaningful connections with other people, the context was always friendships. We are better when we live together in community, we're told. Again, I ask, is that true?

For all the reasons I need to connect with others, I can think of just as many reasons why connecting with others is not worth the risk. Living in community means opening ourselves up to disappointment and pain. I can live without that. Together also means confusion and complexities and awkward comments and giving up my precious time for someone else's agenda. Connecting requires me to first open myself up, which also means making myself vulnerable. You have to be known if you want to know others. Is it worth it?

I have my own answers to these questions, and since the table of contents lists five chapters for this section on connecting with others,

I think you can probably guess where I land. However, we still need to wrestle with these questions if the answers are to have any impact on our lives. I do not want to accept blindly the idea that we need to connect with others because doing so is somehow good for us. All my life I've also been told that eating vegetables is good for me. That didn't make me want to eat lots of veggies. In fact, most of my life it made me feel the opposite way.

I don't know about you, but doing something because it is good for me isn't much of a motivation. What really moves me is discovering not only that something is valuable but also that it is *desirable*. When I can finally connect the dots and discover that a feeling of emptiness I am wrestling with can be satisfied by connecting with others, then I am all in. I won't have to be told that connecting with others is beneficial. If I already hunger for it, I'll pursue it with everything I've got.

But how can we possibly search for answers to these questions when we already have an answer in our minds? My friend, Avery, can tell you.

Avery was born with a rare condition called Russell-Silver syndrome. The medications his doctors prescribed caused Avery to have a stroke at the age of four. Doctors warned his parents he might not live past the age of five. If he somehow managed to survive, doctors did not know if he'd ever walk or talk again. Avery defied the odds and made what looks to be a complete recovery, but he's never been completely what one might call "well." He lives with invisible disabilities. From the outside you'd never know he battles any sort of illness. But he does. Now in his twenties, Avery has spent most of his life in and out of hospitals.

When I first met Avery, he lived in a room at the local children's hospital. You read that right. He *lived* in the hospital. Avery was tangibly in isolation. Disconnected. Cut off. His mother moved a lot of his favorite things into his room and covered the walls with posters. She wanted him to feel at home during the full year he had to stay there, but no number of posters on the wall could change the fact that he was cut off from the rest of the world.

His full year in the hospital also happened to be his senior year of high school. Avery missed it all because—not to be overly dramatic, but it is true—leaving his hospital room would cost him his life. On top of everything else he battled, Avery developed sepsis and a variety of other serious infections. To treat them all, doctors had to place him in complete isolation. Avery described it to me as almost a bubble-boy life. Visitors couldn't come and hang out in his room, and anyone who came into his room, even for a short visit, had to suit up in a full hazmat suit to protect him from any new infections and also to protect them from the infections he was already battling.

Not having visitors wasn't that big of a deal to Avery. He really didn't have any friends. Shy by nature and even more so after growing tired of explaining his invisible disability, he withdrew from most relationships. The other kids in school didn't know he could even talk, since none of his classmates had heard him utter a word since second or third grade. It wasn't just that Avery missed huge blocks of school and was quiet when he was in class. The variety of illnesses he battled all his life created an uncomfortable distance from his classmates. On the outside he didn't look sick, but then he'd miss weeks and months of school. None of his classmates really understood why. And no one wanted to talk about his illnesses.

Russell-Silver syndrome affects the digestive tract, which means

Avery cannot eat like everyone else. If he tries, he'll end up with ulcers and a variety of other complications. But not eating with everyone else in the cafeteria when he looks like everyone else made other kids view him as different. If someone asked why he didn't eat with them, the moment Avery mentioned his illness the questioner changed the subject. People felt uncomfortable talking to him about the one constant in Avery's life. As a result, he started to feel ashamed of a disease he did not choose to be born with and could not control.

The discomfort of others regarding his disabilities made Avery feel uncomfortable about himself. His shame and discomfort built up higher and higher walls until he finally decided doing life alone was a lot less trouble than worrying about friendships. He had his mom and dad, and the staff at the hospital were always nice to him. What more did he need?

I crossed paths with Avery when the children's hospital invited me to come spend an afternoon visiting sick kids. I do these visits every time I'm asked. The hospital brings in lots of people like me, but I didn't know until much later that Avery always turned down the visits. He never cared about having the Broncos cheerleaders come by, nor did he want to see anyone else doing what he calls "the celebrity visits." All that changed when he heard the Bachelor was coming. He's a big fan of the show and, for whatever reason, was actually excited about meeting me.

I didn't know what to expect on this visit to the hospital. I never know how the kids might react to my coming by or even if many will have heard of me. It's not like when a member of the Broncos or the Rockies or the Nuggets goes to the hospital. Kids get really excited about seeing their sports heroes. Me, I'm just an ordinary guy who happened to be on a reality show. However, I love going to visit kids like this. It brings me perspective and gives me a glimpse of a world I do not typically get to see. Even if the kids have no idea who I am, I want to spend time with them and get to know them, which brings me back to Avery.

I noticed Avery's room as soon as I walked onto his hall. Even though a protective barrier had been set up to guard him from visitors' germs, I could see his room looked different. It looked like a teenager's bedroom, not a hospital room. When I asked one of the nurses what was going on with it, she explained to me that Avery had been there for nine straight months. "Avery pretty much lives here," she said. "He can't leave, and he can't have any visitors because he's in isolation."

I had trouble wrapping my head around what I'd just heard. How can anyone spend nine straight months living in a hospital, much less in isolation? He's just a kid! The way the nurse talked it became clear that Avery had spent much of his life in hospitals.

"How old is he?" I asked.

"I think he's seventeen or eighteen," she said. "He's a senior in high school. Ask him to sing," she added. "He can't wait meet you, and he loves to sing. Maybe then he will let his guard down and chat with you, but beware . . . once he starts talking it's hard to get him to stop!"

"What do I need to do to visit him?" I immediately asked. I don't know if I can say that right then I knew visiting Avery was *the* reason I was there that day because I had some good visits with other children as well, but I now realize meeting Avery was a divine appointment.

The nurse explained that, while I couldn't go into his room, I could stand outside the doorway and talk to him through the protective barrier.

"All right. Let's go," I said.

When I walked up to Avery's room, it was like he was waiting for me. I had no idea he was shy because he certainly wasn't with me. We started talking like we'd known each other for a while. In the middle of our visit, Avery said, "Hey, man, did you know I sing?"

"Alright, let's hear it," I said.

Avery then launched into a Johnny Cash song that blew me away.

"How'd you learn to sing like that?" I asked.

Avery laughed. "I don't know, man. I just like to sing."

We talked and joked and laughed together until it was time for me to leave. By the time I left I knew this wasn't just a one-off visit. Avery was a good guy, and I wanted to spend more time hanging out with him. He had a lot to teach me, and I was looking for some more solid friends. I gave him my phone number, and he gave me his. Since that day the two of us have texted back and forth on a regular basis.

Our relationship might never have moved past regular texting if not for a message Avery sent me not long after he got out of the hospital. Because he spent his senior year hospitalized, he missed out on all his senior year milestone events, including his prom. Now Avery was doing his best to make up for what he'd missed. Prom season had rolled back around, and Avery planned to attend. Of course, he wanted his friends to go with him. However, because of his illnesses and his time in the hospital, he didn't know many people at his high school. Aside from his best friend, Dylan, everyone else he even casually knew had graduated the year before, the year Avery missed. That's why he texted me.

"Hey, Ben. Would you go to the prom with me and my other friends? It will be fun."

"Yeah. Why not?" I texted back. Avery then told me about the rest of the group of friends he'd asked to come along with him and his date. These included two players from the Denver Broncos Avery had gotten to know during his stays in the hospital, as well as a couple of our mutual friends who had also appeared on *The Bachelor*.

Attending Avery's prom turned out to be a turning point for the two of us. We became friends that first day when I met him in the hospital. However, after the prom, the two of us started hanging out on a regular basis and built a true friendship. There's nothing I enjoy more than hanging out with him, watching television or going out somewhere for a beer. It's funny, because both of us have had to push back against criticism about our friendship. I've had people assume I am friends with him because he was this sick kid who needed friends, and others assume he is only friends with me because I'm a "celebrity." Neither assumption could be further from the truth. We're friends for the same reason anyone builds a friendship. Both of us like and respect the other and enjoy our time together. We do for one another all the things I talked about in the last chapter. The two of us are friends in the truest sense of the word.

Avery and I never could have built a real friendship if I had looked at him as the "sick kid" rather than as someone who had struggled with disabilities and illness their entire life yet was not defined by them. In some of our earliest conversations, I asked him about his different illnesses and what it was like to put up with them all his life. Avery told me most people usually change the subject the moment his illnesses come up. Me asking him about his condition in a genuine way freed Avery to finally talk about them openly and honestly. The more he opened up about his illnesses, the freer from them he told me he felt. More than that, he started using the illnesses he'd battled and hated and felt embarrassed by his entire life as a means to help and connect with other people. Rather than feeling defeated by his illnesses, he now feels empowered by them. His lifetime as a fighter has given him a way to help other people.

And other people have now become a regular part of Avery's life. In the years since our friendship began at the children's hospital, I've watched Avery become more and more comfortable connecting with other people. He's opened up about his disabilities, even answering people's awkward questions with humor and grace. He's also more open with those he does not know. I guess the shy Avery is still in there somewhere, but I never see it. The man I see is charismatic, funny, likeable, and a leader. When we hang out now, it's hard for me to see someone who used to hang back in the shadows. His is the very definition of a life connected to others, and he does this in a meaningful way.

I don't mean to imply that life is now suddenly easy for Avery. Pain has been a daily reality for my friend his entire life. Some days, he tells me, he feels like he is just existing, not living, because his pain refuses to allow him to think about anything else. Medications might help in the short term, but the results always taper off within a week or two, leaving him right back where he's always been. You see, Avery may look and act like he is better on the outside, but please remember, his invisible disease has not improved.

In summer 2018 Avery flew out to Minnesota for a pain rehab program at the Mayo Clinic. Even though he did his best to remain upbeat, he'd lived with constant pain about as long as he could. He told me he was about ready to give up. The Mayo Clinic Pain Rehabilitation Center (PRC) offered a way to live a good life even though Avery would never be pain-free.

Now here's the part about Avery's experience that showed me how connecting with others has changed his life. He didn't go through the program alone but with twenty other kids his age who had also suffered lifetimes of pain. At first, he shrank back into being the shy kid whose classmates didn't even realize could talk. As the thirty-day program progressed, however, he started opening up and talking honestly about his experience with pain. By the time the month ended, he'd built solid relationships and true friendships. Becoming vulnerable is never easy or comfortable, but Avery pushed through and connected with people in a way he probably would not have just a couple of years earlier.

All of this brings me back to the questions I asked at the beginning of this chapter: Are we really better together? Do friendships and honest connections with people truly enhance our lives? For Avery and me, the answer to both has to be yes. I know my life is better because of our friendship, and he says the same about me. Connecting with others in a meaningful, significant way has drastically improved his life, he told me. And he would know because he's lived on both sides of the equation, although not by choice. He presents the perfect before and after scenario.

Today, if you ask him if we truly are better together, he'll smile and give you an enthusiastic yes. I think he speaks for all of us. My life is better because of friends like Avery. I'm not sure how anyone can quantify the value of a friendship. For me, all I can say is I cannot imagine living without them.

CHAPTER 6

What's It All About?

If you haven't noticed already, I enjoy asking questions (probably because I know very little). The question I've asked myself more than any other is one of the most common questions of human existence: What is this life all about?

The question has been thrown around since the beginning of time, but that doesn't mean we have a lot of good answers. Of course, there's the religious answer, the one you hear at church. There the answer is easy: Jesus. I get that, but that's not the question I'm asking. I want to know what will make this life matter to the degree that, when I get to the end of my life and I'm on my deathbed, I won't look back and say, "I thought there was more."

I'm not asking what will make me the happiest. Just because something makes me happy doesn't make it good for me. Stuffing my face with pizza and beer can make me happy, but I don't need a lifetime of that. No, what I really want to know is, how can I invest the finite amount of time I've been given in a way that will leave me saying at the end, "This was good and this was well done"? The earlier in life I can discover the answer, the longer I have to enjoy its fruit, which gives this quest a great sense of urgency.

Urgency is what I felt not that long ago when I didn't know if my dad would live or die. A week earlier he'd come to Denver to help me reroof my house. Even though he was nearly sixty at the time, my dad has always been such a high-energy, get-things-done kind of guy, and I couldn't think of anyone I'd rather have help me on the project. More than anything, I just wanted to spend time with him. But my dad wasn't himself during this trip. He moved slower than usual and grew tired more quickly. At night he went to bed early, and in the morning I had to wake him up, which was a role reversal for us. Both of us noticed, but neither of us thought too much about it. "I guess I'm not as young as I used to be," my dad joked. I never thought there could be any more to it than that.

A couple of days after my dad flew home to Indiana, my mom called me. "Ben, you need to get home. Your dad has a 99 percent blockage in three arteries in his heart. They've scheduled him for a triple bypass. I think . . . I think you need to be here before he goes in for surgery."

I understood my mom was implying more than she was saying. This wasn't my father's first brush with death. As I mentioned in the introduction, he was diagnosed with stage four cancer when my mother was pregnant with me. She nearly lost him then. Thankfully he was able to make a complete recovery. However, the type of chemo they used to combat my dad's cancer weakened his internal organs.

When I was a junior in high school, doctors discovered my dad's heart was enlarged and dying as a direct result of his cancer treatments years earlier. They didn't expect him to survive. Three times that year my father handed me a blue folder and told me it contained everything I needed to know in case he didn't make it. The blue folder is now symbolic and a tangible reminder of the fragility of life. My dad still updates it at least once a year. It holds all the important documents and details about finances, health care, assets, family history, and everything else I might need to transition into a life without my father. Thankfully, I didn't need the folder any of those times, and my father survived his heart issues then. Now I understood that his previous health issues made his odds of surviving this new round of heart problems much lower. My dad had handed that blue folder to me so many times when I was in high school, and I did not look forward to receiving it again.

I booked a flight and immediately flew back to Indiana. A million thoughts and emotions ran through my head during that flight and on the drive from the airport to the hospital. I thought about what I wanted to say to my dad, knowing this could be our last conversation. I also needed to be strong for my mom. I found myself praying constantly, even when I wasn't conscious that I was praying. We'd come so close to losing my dad before that I did not want to presume God was going to save him again. Of course, that's still how I wanted this to turn out. I wanted us all to keep living happily ever after, but I'd already had ten years more with my father than doctors thought we'd have. Thinking back to the stories my mom told me about my dad's cancer, I felt lucky I'd had any time with him at all.

By the time I walked into my dad's hospital room, I'd managed to get my emotions under control, sort of. I sat down next to his hospital bed and took his hand. Above, the television was on. The Cubs were playing the Pirates. Looking up at the game on TV made this moment with my dad seem less odd. I can't tell you how many Cubs games my dad and I had watched together on television or how many times we'd gone to Wrigley Field. The game played on. The two of us talked about how he felt and about the next day's surgery and how my trip was, but I kept thinking, *If this is the last moment I have with my dad, what do I want this moment to be?*

And then it hit me how incredibly lucky I was to even be there with him and to get to ask that question. Not many people get a final moment with those they love. But I might. The gravity of the moment, knowing this might be my final night with my father, created an urgency and an intentionality to connect I could not take for granted. There's something uniquely transcendent about truly connecting with another person, family or not, especially when you think this could be your last time together. And that's all I wanted to do in that moment. I wanted to be fully present, to soak up this time with my father, even if all we did was watch the Cubs together and talk about the game. I would have wanted it no other way.

It's funny. When we start out watching a movie or reading a book, we have no clue where the story will take us. Life is the same. When we are still alive, we have no clue what the next page or scene will bring. It isn't until the book or movie ends that we look back on the entire story and realize what each chapter meant. The moments when we feel like the story may be over are when we are able to look back and see what was learned, appreciated, and valued. That's what this conversation with my dad gave me. I thank God for it. I also thank him that my father's story still has chapters left to write.

The Answer to the Big Question

That night in the hospital did not turn out to be my last night with my dad. Once again, he came through his surgery and made a full recovery. After it was all over, I kept thinking back on that night and the urgency I felt to truly connect with him. The time we spent together wasn't about ball games or accomplishments, or my work or stressors or anything other than being fully present and making every second intentional and focused. If that night had been the end, I imagine I would have still felt a heavy and overwhelming sadness, but those last moments would have still been filed in my memory bank as "good."

Reflecting back on the experience makes me think that this is the answer to the question I asked at the beginning of this chapter: What is this life all about? What makes it worth living? What makes our days worthwhile? What keeps moments with others from being just a way to pass time? The answer lies in connecting with people. Life matters most when shared, both the joys and the pains, the profound moments as well as the most ordinary. That's what connecting looks like. It is being present without having an agenda, loving another both at their best and their worst.

Connecting means risking vulnerability and building each other up through encouragement. To connect is to see and to be seen, to let each other know that we are not alone and never will be, even when we're absent from one another. Life still takes place without it, but the connections we make with others give fulfillment and joy and satisfaction and clarity. For many people, this realization does not come until their life is about to end. As the old saying goes, no one on their deathbeds ever said they wished they'd spent more time at the office. For me, I don't want to wait that long to figure this out. I want to begin living for connections now.

Life is not about the next sale. It's not about the next promotion or the next dollar or the next house or the next car or the next great escapade. Real life has always been found in looking around you and participating in other people's stories, pouring yourself into them, giving to them more than they give to you. If my dad had not survived his bypass operation, the greatest gifts he would have left me would have been the time we spent together and the impact he made on my life. Of course, you can say, "Sure you'd say that, Ben. He's your dad." But the same is true for everyone in my life. It's the connections that matter, and the impact, good and bad, that we make upon one another.

Thinking about this makes me ask, *If this is true, then what are we waiting for?* If our connections with others give this life meaning, it's time for us to wake up and start investing our lives in what matters now. I understand that what I'm saying here is nothing new or revolutionary. I understand and expect these lessons to be just reminders to us all. However, there is a disconnect between what we say is most important and what we actually invest our days doing. If the connections we make are what matter most, then today is the best time to begin being fully present in the lives of others, not for what they can do for us but for what we can do for them!

We live in what I believe to be the most isolated time in history, and that will not change as long as we hold back. Our only hope is for each of us to become intentional and begin connecting with others in a meaningful way.

The Hard Part

That last couple of paragraphs were easy to write, but actually making these kinds of connections is not. It's not like there's a formula to instantly create meaningful relationships. You cannot force them to happen. In reality, I think all any of us can really do is lay the groundwork and open ourselves up for them.

Not long ago I sat with a friend I'd made in a village in Honduras. She's only twenty-two, but she already has four children and has lived a very hard life. Like me, her dad was diagnosed with cancer when she was young, but her story did not have a happy ending. After her father discovered he had testicular cancer, he set out to leave a lasting legacy for his family. From the day he was diagnosed until he became too sick to work, he spent every waking hour building a house to leave behind for his wife and children. He so wanted to leave a roof over their heads that he literally worked himself to death on that house. In the end, my friend's father felt satisfied that he'd given his best gift to them, the gift of safety and security. The gesture was appreciated and from an outside perspective very honorable, but my friend told me she'd rather have had that time with her father, especially with the way her life turned after his death.

When my friend's father died, her mother was so shaken by grief that she could not step foot inside the house he'd devoted his last few months to building. Everything in it reminded her of him and the pain of losing him. Rather than the house becoming a place of shelter for his family, the mother ended up selling it immediately, then leaving with the money. My friend, who was just a young girl at the time, was left to fend for herself. A family in the village took her in and allowed her to live with them and go to school up through the end of elementary school. Once she finished the sixth grade, though, the family kicked her out. Apparently, they thought she was old enough to take care of herself. She ended up getting married at the age of fourteen, only to have her husband abandon her and take their child north to the United States, where he was from. Eventually she remarried and had more children, but her life is still filled with sadness.

As she told me her story, I felt the depth of what she was telling me. The two of us have been friends for two years. Over that time, we've broken bread together and celebrated birthdays together and become what I considered to be good friends. But her moment of vulnerability, when she opened up and told me her story for the first time, connected us in a way we never had before. For the first time I felt like I truly knew her. She did not tell me her story for me to magically try and fix anything. She simply wanted to be heard and understood, and I felt very privileged that she'd entrusted me with that responsibility.

Reflecting on that conversation, I see the essence of what a meaningful connection looks like: Vulnerability. Trust. Presence. Selflessness. Listening without judging. Being present without feeling the need to speak up and "fix" what the other is going through.

Yet I found there were moments as my friend poured out her heart to me that I struggled to reciprocate. I had trouble being fully present and selfless. As she told me what she'd gone through, I thought about how I would feel if I had gone through this myself. I found myself thinking about how blessed I am and how fortunate I am to have never experienced homelessness or the losses she has tasted multiple times. Before I realized it, I was thinking only of myself, not my friend. I started to focus on what I felt as she told me her story rather than focusing on her and being fully present with her. In this conversation, which was 100 percent not about me, I started to make it about me, and when I did, the connection was lost. More than anything, she needed to be heard and, in my listening, I stopped hearing her.

Looking back, I realize how difficult it is to connect with others because the self has a way of trying to jump in the way. The root of selfishness that lies deep within us all too often finds a way to bring the conversation back around to the question: What's in it for me? But connecting with others is not something that can be quantified in those terms. The moment I enter into a relationship thinking solely about how it will benefit me, I slam the door on connecting. As soon as I start making our interactions about me, I become disconnected from the purpose of these connections. But when my focus is on the other person, on being there for their benefit and not mine, I then become the best version of myself and end up benefiting in ways I never could on my own.

If it all sounds a little confusing, it is. The whole idea is completely counterintuitive. The benefit of connecting with others can only be experienced when my focus is on benefiting others and not myself. I know this is a little hard to wrap your head around. Perhaps the best way to explain it is to show you a picture of it in action.

What a Friend We Have . . .

When I started doing research for this section of the book, I spent a lot of time reading and thinking about Jesus' relationship with his disciples. Sometimes it's easy for us to lose sight of the fact that Jesus came to the earth as completely human. More than that, I don't always appreciate how small his window of time on this earth actually was. Luke 3:23 tells us that Jesus was about thirty years old when he started his ministry. That statement really jumps out at me because I turned thirty right before I started writing this book. Then, when Jesus was around thirty-three, the work was over and that was it. The Son of God, sent to earth to change the course of human history, did all he came to earth to do in just three years. And his primary way of doing so wasn't through the miracles he performed or the sermons he preached. Instead, Jesus spent the vast majority of his time here on earth investing in the lives of other people. And he didn't invest that time in the kings and queens of the earth. He spent most of his time with the outcasts: the tax collectors and the poor and the diseased and prostitutes and every other sort of sinner.

When I think about the connections Jesus made with people, I don't see much benefit for him personally. His disciples, his closest group of friends, let him down time after time, but he never gave up on them. Peter, perhaps Jesus' best friend, three times denied he even knew Jesus. I cannot help but think about how it would feel for me to hear one of my closest friends deny our relationship. Then there were James and John, the other two who, along with Peter, formed Jesus' inner circle. They came to him one day and asked if they could sit on his right and left sides when he set up his kingdom. That is, they wanted *the* most important spots for themselves. Their request was the very definition of "what's in it for me," but Jesus didn't get mad at them over it. The other ten disciples did, but Jesus didn't. He was patient and told them that they didn't understand what they were asking for, then reminded them that serving others, not being served, is the highest calling of all (Mark 10:35–45).

I see the same patience in the connections Jesus made with people who weren't part of the twelve disciples. One of my favorite stories is the one where Jesus was walking through Jericho and everyone in town turned out to try to get a glimpse of him. One man was too short to see over the crowd, a man named Zacchaeus. The Bible says Zacchaeus wasn't just any man. He was the chief tax collector in the region, and he was very rich. He became rich because he overcharged people on their taxes and pocketed the difference. That made him one of the most despised people in all of Jericho. And yet, it was Zacchaeus whom Jesus sought out to spend time with one-on-one. Jesus actually invited himself to be a guest in Zacchaeus's house, which was the ultimate sign of acceptance. Choosing to spend time with Zacchaeus didn't help Jesus in any way. In fact, he made everyone else in town angry because he chose to be a "guest of a notorious sinner" (Luke 19:7). All the giving in this relationship came from Jesus' side, but that was Jesus' intent and the example he gave us to follow.

Jesus loved the outsider. He also loved the oppressed, the sick, and the hurting. The people who had nothing to give back to him. The people it would seem he had no reason to befriend, as it would be of no benefit to him. But he still loved them. He dove deep into connection with people who had a story to share, and like most of us, that story oftentimes included tears and pain. Jesus sat next to those tears and pains—it didn't matter if the person could justify their hurt or feelings of oppression, Jesus did not let his own agenda get in the way of hearing from the hurting. It seems to me that if someone felt oppressed, then, to Jesus, they were oppressed and it was his responsibility to sit alongside that oppression. And he even eventually took on the position of being oppressed himself. Followers of Christ watched their leader mocked, beaten, humiliated, and then crucified on a cross. Christianity does not have roots in victory. Instead, it has roots in brokenness, laying down one's life, and resurrection. And we, as present-day followers of this savior, are called to the same.

As James H. Cone said it,

> The Christian community, therefore, is that community that freely becomes oppressed, because they know that Jesus himself has defined humanity's liberation in the context of what happens to the little ones. Christians join the cause of the oppressed in the fight for justice not because of some philosophical principle of "the Good" or because of a religious feeling of sympathy for people in prison. Sympathy does not change the structures of injustice. The authentic identity of Christians with the poor is found in the claim which the Jesus-encounter lays upon their own life-style, a claim that connects the word "Christian" with the liberation of the poor. Christians fight not for humanity in general but for themselves and out of their love for concrete human beings.[5]

As we see the tearstained faces and choose to listen to those whose stories are rooted in pain, the way Jesus did, there comes a desire to ask, "How can I help?" This question manifests not because it benefits us but because it is authentically Christian to love others and fight injustice in ways people unaffected by Jesus would not. Let us lay our bodies down at the foot of the cross and at the feet of those who need us most. That is how we live a life that matters.

Life matters when we spend it connecting with others, but we can only connect when we're operating on a level where our focus is on pouring ourselves into others, not on what people are giving us. As we do, we operate as the best versions of ourselves. Conversely, when we set out with a "What's in it for me?" mindset, there's nothing in it for us. There is no true connection or lasting benefit. In the words of Jesus, I lose my life, then I gain it. It's all counterintuitive, but it's the only way to find what really matters—to make the kinds of connections that allow us, at the end, to look back and say, "It was all worth it. This was what life was supposed to be all about."

CHAPTER 7

The Bridge

A few weeks before I started writing this book, my cousin called and asked if I could come help her summer community theater group with their production of *Grease*. She'd been a part of this group since the first grade and now, as a senior in high school, this was going to be her last year. My heart sank a little when she asked. To be completely honest, it was hard for me to imagine getting excited about spending a week in Marion, Indiana, doing the musical *Grease* with a group of high school students. But for whatever reason, I knew I'd regret it if I turned her down. Like me, she's felt like an outsider most of her life. Even without voicing it to each other, I can see in her eyes that she understands my insecurities because they are hers as well. For her, this theater group was the one place where she felt like people got her. That's why, when she asked me to come help, I couldn't tell her no, no matter how hard I tried to convince myself I could.

My week with the group went much better than I expected. But the most important moment for me came on the last day. I walked into the theater and found all the seniors standing in a big circle, their arms wrapped around one another. Their last show was about to start, which made this their final huddle before they went out on stage. Outwardly, the students in the circle could not have been more different: girls, boys, gay, straight, black, white, Asian. Yet, in spite of their outward differences, this group had become a family. Now they were about to say goodbye for perhaps the final time. At the end of that night's performance, they'd all pack up and go off to different colleges and perhaps never see one another again. Of course, they could keep up with each other on social media, but that's not the same.

Everyone in the circle felt the weight of the moment. Tears flowed. The more they cried, the tighter they hugged one another. No one could bring themselves to talk until one guy finally said, "Nobody knows me like you guys know me."

"This is the first place I've never felt judgment," another said. "I love all of you."

"I've never felt more accepted than I have by this group," another said.

"I don't know what I'm going to do without you," someone said, which was immediately met with a chorus of "Me too."

I didn't say anything for a while. Instead, I listened not only to what they were saying but why they said it. I've heard the same sentiments with other groups in their final farewells to one another. Saying goodbye to those who actually get you is one of the hardest moments in life. When you already feel like an outsider, the thought of being separated from the one place where you feel like you belong is scary. Just connecting with a group takes so much effort, so much vulnerability, that the thought of having to do it again intimidates us. A lot of people can't bring themselves to try.

As you have picked up so far, I believe that human beings connect through shared experiences, especially those where you have to work together to accomplish something you could never do on your own. This group obviously had that through all the summers they came together to put on theater productions. But the words they used to describe how this group had impacted them went beyond working together. Most sounded like they were a lot like my cousin. Outside of this group, they felt like they did not belong. They battled loneliness and isolation, along with hurt and disappointment and feeling insignificant. Most expressed how they didn't fit in anywhere else, like they didn't matter. In this theater group they found kindred spirits who shared their pain and connected through it.

As the kids in the circle hugged each other tighter and cried even more, I witnessed a type of vulnerability most people do everything they can to avoid. We may feel hurt and misunderstood, but most of us don't want to admit those feelings to a group, especially not with tears. We overcompensate and joke and act like we're fine, like nothing bothers us, while on the inside we're dying. The kids in this circle had dropped all their masks and were completely real with one another. That's why they felt so connected. As long as we act like we have it all together, we'll never connect. But once we drop the act, once we allow ourselves to be honest with others who understand what we're going through because they've gone through it themselves, that's when we feel the closest to each other.

Finally, I spoke up. "You have just expressed everything that makes this community so beautiful. All the things that have allowed you to connect on a level you've never connected with another human in your life; all the things that have allowed you to feel loved and accepted and trusted and safe. This is beautiful. And I know you all are scared because you don't know what the next stage of life is going to bring. I know you are hurting because you do not want to lose the connections you have in this room right now.

"But," I continued, "instead of mourning what may be about to end, you should celebrate it. You should tell one another thank you for teaching what true love looks like, what true community looks like, what true connection looks like. I know none of you know what the future may hold, but I want to challenge you to take what you've learned from this circle of people and go and create this in every season of your life, no matter where you may go. No matter who you are with. No matter if it is one person or eight. Be the community starter. You know how. Think about what connected you here. It wasn't just the productions you pulled off. More than that, it's how you connected over your hurts and your vulnerabilities. You took time to get to know one another and love each other. I know from experience that many people in this world feel completely disconnected and misunderstood. They need a group like this. Because you have been taught connection through this group, you can take the first steps to connect with them."

I don't know how many people in that circle went on to become community builders, but my words for them are really the main thing I want you to take away from this book. This section, connecting with others, isn't about what others should do for you but what you should do for them. The most isolated time in human history needs people to be community builders. It has to start with someone. Why not us? Why not you? It's easy to sit back and wonder why no one cares about me and how nobody wants to connect with me. That's the victim mindset we talked about a few chapters ago, and it's nothing more than an excuse. We have to start creating community on our own.

The big question is, *How can I build a bridge and connect with others?* I witnessed firsthand the answer in my cousin's theater group. We connect through shared experiences, and no experience is stronger than shared pain. It's also the one constant, the one universal that can build a bridge with anyone we meet. By pain, I am not referring only to physical pain. I'm talking about the emotional hurts we all endure as we go through life.

Everyone gets hurt. Everyone struggles with disappointment. Everyone experiences loss. Everyone wrestles with times of feeling insignificant. Everyone tastes sorrow at some point in their life. If you have not, I'm really happy for you but I have to warn you: your turn will come because it comes for everyone. I wish it didn't, but it does. Pain, along with death (fun thought, huh?), is the one constant for every human being. That's why it can connect us, even when we have nothing else in common.

But pain by itself cannot build a bridge. We all experience pain, yet that doesn't automatically make us connect. To connect through our pain, we must first be authentic. Brené Brown described this as letting go of who we think we should be in order to be who we are.[6] This was very much the goal of the first section of this book on reconnecting with yourself. Until you reconnect with yourself, it is difficult to connect with others. That reconnection means we stop looking down on ourselves, stop talking about how we've fallen short or how we aren't good enough or smart enough or *enough* enough and embrace this person God loves.

Connecting through pain also requires vulnerability. I find this to be the point where many people walk away. The dictionary defines *vulnerability* as being exposed to the possibility of being attacked or harmed, either physically or emotionally. That's the place where it loses most of us. No one wants to leave themselves open to attack, especially those who have been attacked in the past. Our lack of vulnerability often shows up in our overcompensating in other parts of our lives. Instead of admitting our weaknesses, we make a show of how strong we are. Brown described this as going through life with the attitude of, "I'm right, you're wrong. Shut up."[7] We don't let ourselves open up to one another. We muscle our way through life, and when we do feel pain, we cover it with blame. It's always someone else's fault, not ours, even when it is completely our own fault.

I learned all this the hard way.

Several years ago, I went through a period of about four months where I was completely disconnected from everyone. I could barely get out of bed, much less interact with others. I wasn't just depressed. I was ashamed. I'd made a huge mess not only of my life but of the lives of others. I felt so bad that I retreated deep inside myself because I was afraid I was going to hurt somebody again. I didn't trust myself. I didn't like myself, let alone love myself.

I didn't arrive at this place overnight. It all began, innocently enough, when I hurt my knee during a high school football game. I knew the injury was bad, but I didn't realize how bad until two surgeries later. Even then my knee hurt constantly. The doctors prescribed painkillers, and I soon found myself addicted. I knew I needed to get off of them, but I found it hard to do when, after every surgery, I was prescribed them again. In addition, a lot of the people I chose to hang out with at this stage of my life were also taking painkillers.

Getting off the painkillers became even more difficult when a different kind of pain hit. I'd applied to one of the top business schools in the country, but they turned me down cold. I kept telling myself to bounce over to plan B, but I couldn't. I could only see one path to success, and now it was closed to me. Instead of picking myself up and moving forward, I pretty much just gave up. The pills numbed my shame and failure. Take a pill, lie in bed, wait until the feeling went away, and once the feeling came back . . . repeat.

Around that same time, a girl I'd dated for a year and a half unceremoniously dumped me. That's not exactly right. She didn't just dump me. I walked in on her making out with another guy. Then she dumped me. Looking back at where I was in life, I can't blame her, but at the time that was just one more confirmation of my loser status in life.

On top of it all my dad was sick again, and I had no idea how that was going to turn out. Rather than face my fears, I hid inside my addiction, which just kept this circle moving faster and faster. I guess I could have prayed, but by then I had pretty much given up on prayer and everything connected to the faith I claimed to have when I was younger. Something inside of me couldn't completely abandon the idea of God, but I'd dropped everything I'd ever connected to him. Church. Prayer. Meditation. The Bible. Belief. I'd tossed them all aside for a variety of reasons—none of them good. I thought I'd just become too smart and too jaded for the things of God.

The final piece of my dark puzzle fell into place when I started to treat people like objects that existed for my pleasure. As much as I hate to admit it now, I never felt bad about doing this until I finally hurt one person too many. I don't want to go into too much detail, but suffice it to say, I used a young woman as nothing more than an object for my pleasure. When it was over, I discarded her. I didn't care about her story or her desire for a relationship that wasn't just physical and lasted longer than one night. I didn't care that I'd hurt her. All I cared about was myself. My need was greater than hers. I only wanted what I wanted, and I saw her as little more than a way for me to get it. And when I had that, we were done. I went off in search of my next object. Little did I know that when we treat people like objects, it always leads to pain.

And the pain eventually came. For her it was immediate. For me it took longer, but once it hit, it hit hard, and I deserved every bit of it. I tried to hide what I'd done, then I tried to hide from those I'd disappointed. But in the end there was no hiding. I found that I could not hide from the one person who was the most disappointed, not only by what I'd done but by what I'd become, and that was me. I hid in bed as much as I could, only dragging myself out into the world when absolutely necessary. I got to a point where my life revolved around shame and disappointment and grief and fear. I had hurt so many people—I was a bulldozer of pain. Hiding allowed me to hurt only myself, but it also plunged me deeper and deeper into myself and deeper into the shame and disappointment and grief and fear.

Everything came to a head one morning. To be honest, looking back I do not remember many mornings during this long period of bedridden shame and darkness. However, I do remember this morning. I dragged myself out of bed and stumbled into the bathroom. I looked into the mirror, hoping to see some sign of life in my eyes. When I made eye contact with myself, I felt like the devil himself was staring back at me. "Oh, God," I said out loud. "Who is this? This is not the man I ever wanted to be." I really meant the words, "Oh, God."

It was the first prayer I'd prayed in a very long time—and maybe the most honest prayer I'd ever uttered. I didn't say these words in vain or even as a reaction but as a way of crying out to God for help. "God, please save me from the man I have become and am becoming."

My pride tried to hold on to the idea that I could fix myself, but by now I knew better. I had to get help. I could not make it unless God intervened, which is what I asked him to do. On my own I had not found any way to move beyond the darkness—only addiction, numbing, and disconnection. I confessed to God how empty my life had become and how I did not want to stay on this path. "If you are real," I cried, "save me from myself."

I believe in that moment God took my darkness. However, the drastic change from darkness to light made me, well, annoying. For the next few months I became the classic overly passionate, probably more than a little obnoxious, newborn believer. During that summer I went back to my hometown, where I started Bible studies for college kids and anyone else who might want to come. Around 150 people signed up, and we averaged somewhere around 70 to 80 people each week. To me this was the proof that I'd turned a corner. Instead of hiding in my bed, I was talking about God with a lot of people.

The Bible study, constant preaching to others (whether they asked for it or not), and my sense of moral superiority kept me from confronting the circumstances that had plunged me into my dark place in the first place. Instead of hiding in my bed and succumbing to depression, I now hid inside my zeal for God. Even though I interacted with people, I was still disconnected. When people shared their problems with me, I didn't listen. Instead I was a fixer, the guy with a Bible verse handy for every situation. Have a problem? Just plug in the right verse and everything will be all right. Fixers aren't connectors and never will be until they stop trying to fix pain and share it instead, but I was a long way from learning that lesson.

I also tried to make amends with the people I'd hurt, but a simple "I'm sorry" and "I'm a changed man" could not mend every hurt. Seeing the lasting effects of what I'd done amplified the guilt that had driven me to my knees before God to begin with. Deep inside, I still felt a disconnect between the person I was and the man I'd always hoped to be. I felt ashamed, like I'd blown it to such a degree that even though I knew God had forgiven me, I'd always be stuck in a less-than life. Yet, as a Bible study leader, I felt like I had to act as if I had my life together.

Thankfully, a friend called me in the middle of that summer and asked me to meet him for coffee. We talked about the changes that had taken place in my life. I tried to keep up the "everything's better with Jesus" facade, but he wasn't buying it. Instead of condemning me for my past or rebuking me for not having enough faith to make my mistakes go away completely, he listened and engaged with me. He asked honest questions that eventually forced me to get honest with him. I told him how I still carried the disappointment of failing to get accepted into business school and how my dad's illness weighed heavily upon me, and I opened up about the weight of the shame from how I'd hurt people. My friend listened patiently until I was pretty much talked out. I felt very small sitting across from him, like a failure who had been given a second chance, but still a failure.

"Think about everything you just told me, Ben," my friend said. "I want you to think about all the things, big and small, that have brought you to this point, especially all the negatives you just told me about. Don't you see how these have all worked together to bring you to this point, right now, today? You talked a lot about your dad's illness and how that weighs on you. I know it does, but it has also produced a determination in you that has changed the way you see the world. You can now look beyond a lot of the junk people get so caught up in. And the relationships you've messed up, I'd be worried if you didn't feel as bad about them as you do. But you don't have to repeat those mistakes. I know you won't. Because of what you've done in the past, you are now free to open yourself up to new relationships that will be very different."

I'd never thought about my past in this way. The bad parts, the things I wish had never happened to me, as well as the things I wish I'd never done, can actually enhance my life. That seemed like a radically uncomfortable idea. Yet the evidence was sitting right across from me. My friend used my pain to connect with me. All I had to do was get real and open myself up for it to happen. As a result, I walked away from that conversation feeling free.

Crossing the Bridge

Your pain and shame and guilt and disappointments and feelings of insignificance, or whatever it is you wrestle with, have the potential to be the bridge you can use to connect with others. That's why I just shared my story with you, so that we can connect in a way we haven't thus far in this book. After reading my story, you may conclude that I am a horrible person, and you are right. I was. Thankfully my story didn't end with the ugly parts. I hope that you will now love me authentically because you know about this part of my story. How beautiful it would be if you did. Having you reject me when you learned some ugly truth about me is a risk I took.

I know dropping your guard and opening up can be frightening. It is easy to love people at their best, but what happens when you have to love someone at their worst? This gets real when you have to choose to love another as you gain a clear view of their mistakes, their quirks, and their differences and choose to see the beauty in their story.

Crossing the bridge of pain is not a simple thing. The beauty of bridges is that they come in all shapes and sizes. Some bridges are wide and easy to cross, but the bridge of pain built with authenticity and vulnerability looks a lot like the Mackinac Bridge in northern Michigan, five miles long and crossing the Straits of Mackinac where Lakes Michigan and Huron come together. From a distance the bridge looks huge, like a green Golden Gate Bridge. But when you get up on it, you find it's a really narrow, four-lane bridge with no shoulders and low, see-through guardrails. As if that's not bad enough, the two center lanes are made of steel grate, which means you can look right through and see the water two hundred feet below. The Mackinac Bridge is so frightening that drivers have been known to panic in the middle and just stop their cars completely. With no confidence to keep going, they just stop. Frozen. Stuck. That's why the bridge authority has drivers available to drive you across the bridge while you hide your eyes in the back seat. A helper in a sense, the drivers have driven over it many times before. They know the bridge well, and they will meet you where you are and help you cross. However, for those brave souls willing to go across, the views from the top are amazing. And there's really no other way to get to the other side without taking a nine-hundred-mile detour around the whole of Lake Michigan.

Building a bridge through your pain can be just as scary, but believe me, the effort is well worth it. Bridges connect people, and when you connect via shared pain through authenticity and vulnerability, the connections you make will change your life forever. And while you are on the bridge, if you can take a moment and look around, you just might find a view that is stunningly beautiful.

CHAPTER 8

Breaking Out of the Bubble

I grew up in a bubble, but I didn't know it at the time. Nearly everyone I hung out with in my hometown looked alike and talked alike and had similar families with parents who probably voted alike. My friends and I all watched the same television shows and listened to the same music and cheered for the same sports teams. Most of us went to church and, with one exception, those who didn't still self-identified as Christian as opposed to Jewish or Muslim or another world religion.

Don't get me wrong. I love and appreciate my hometown. The people I love the most still live there. I'm not criticizing my hometown when I say that it didn't boast a lot of diversity. Very few small towns around the world do. I knew from watching television and reading books that people were different around the globe, but while I knew this to be true in my mind, I never experienced it myself. I always just sort of assumed that my bubble was a microcosm of what life was like for everybody, even those who didn't look like me or talk like me.

My first memory of contact with the world outside of my bubble occurred one July when a group came into a church service wearing matching neon-colored T-shirts. Our pastor announced that this group had just returned from a mission trip to Honduras. The leader of the group shared stories from their trip, and afterward everyone told the group what a great work they had done. The next week another group came in wearing their matching neon T-shirts, and another came the next week, and the next. Every summer at my church, four different mission teams would each set out on a one-week trip. I joined in with the rest of the church as we prayed for the teams in the weeks before T-shirt Sundays. The work in Honduras was important, we were told, maybe even dangerous, which is why we prayed so hard for each team.

I was always fascinated by the work of those who went down to Honduras in their matching neon T-shirts. I wanted to know more about what they did down there. As soon as I was old enough to join a team, I started trying to talk my parents into going as a family. The work sounded a little too dangerous for me to go all by myself, yet I badly wanted to be a part of it. Eventually my parents and their small group (church language for friends who confide in each other as adults) all decided it was a good idea to join a T-shirt team, and we were on our way. In preparation for the trip we attended lots of meetings where we were given a long list of safety concerns. The country was poor, we were told, and dangerous, potentially very dangerous! I told myself that's why we were going, because these people needed our help. We had a lot to offer, I believed. We were the saviors. I liked that idea, and to be honest, I also liked the idea of getting a pat on the back when we returned, even if it meant lots of immunization shots before we left.

I finally received my neon T-shirt right before we left for Honduras. Our team's shirts were all bright pink with the mission organization's name across the front. We had to wear them in the airport and on the plane and in Honduras as we traveled to our team hotel. The mission team leaders herded us about, making sure everyone was where they were supposed to be, when they were supposed to be there, lest kidnappers single out one of us "rich" Americans and hold us for ransom. Keeping us together kept everyone safe. In a way the trip felt a lot like an eighth-grade class trip. This was less a mission trip and more of a field trip for adults, although I'd never had a field trip where armed military guards rode along on our team bus. I took one look at the guards and their guns and wished I'd stayed in Indiana. All of the safety meetings now made sense. We truly were risking our lives, I thought.

The first night at our team's hotel, we started prepping for the next day, our first day in the field. Fear ran through my veins. All I really wanted to do was go home. No neon T-shirt was worth risking my life. A pat on the back would be nice, but I could get that by shoveling my grandparents' snowy driveway and telling my mom what I did. I looked over at my mom and dad, and it hit me that everyone I loved the most was on this trip and at risk. In Matthew 16:18, Jesus said the gates of hell will not prevail against his church. *Well, Jesus, I hope you are right.* I felt like we were about to put that statement to the test.

And then we went to the first village.

The plan was for us to hand out about a month's worth of rice and beans and cooking oil to the villagers, along with some used clothing, in partnership with a disaster relief organization. After we passed out the food and clothes, we were to hold a church service before going on to another village, where we'd pass out more food and clothes and have church before heading off to another village and another after that. The whole idea was to provide some short-term physical relief and perhaps introduce the villagers to Jesus. After a week of going from village to village, we'd go home to Indiana and walk into church in our matching neon pink shirts to share our battle stories. After that, we'd return to our normal lives until the next mission trip season rolled around.

At least that was the plan. Fifteen years later I can tell you the plan didn't work out so well for me.

I thought I knew what to expect when our bus pulled into the first village, but I was wrong. We'd been told that the village was poor, but this kid who'd grown up in the bubble of small-town, middle-class America had no idea what poor meant until it slapped me in the face. Not to diminish or undervalue the people of that village, but my first impression when we pulled in was that these people lived in trash. Their homes, these shacks, appeared to be made out of plastic bags and whatever else people had salvaged from the dump to turn into a place to live. The children running out of the shacks appeared to be filthy, with sores on their bodies and stick-thin arms and legs.

When we stepped off the bus, the smell rising up from the toilets, which were nothing more than holes in the ground, nearly knocked me over. I watched some women draw water from the river that flowed not more than twenty yards from the hole-in-the-ground toilets. Flies buzzed all around me as our team leader told us to take our positions to start the food distribution. I had a hard time concentrating. I looked all around, and as far as my eye could see, there was nothing but more trash shacks and more sick children and more flies. There weren't any beautiful buildings off on the horizon to give a sense of hope that maybe a better life was possible. The people of this village lived in true poverty on a scale I didn't think was possible. My bubble, out of nowhere and within seconds, had been unexpectedly burst.

After a week of traveling from one impoverished village to another, I no longer cared about being patted on the back for all the good work I'd done. Good work meant I made a difference, and I couldn't see how we'd done anything more than pour water on sand. I felt guilty about the life I went back to when we returned to our team hotel each night. Guilt became a kind of running joke with our team. We asked one another if we were supposed to feel bad about drinking clean water and taking hot showers and sleeping in soft beds in air-conditioned rooms. A few people talked about how we should be more thankful for our lives back home, but I had trouble doing that. But I felt angry and confused, like my entire life up to that point had been a lie. More than anything I was mad at God, because here were people suffering without a solution. No matter how many boxes of rice and beans and oil we handed out, these people were still not going to have clean water or any sort of hope for a better future.

How could God let that happen? I'd joined a team to go down to Honduras as a savior, as someone bringing gifts that would make me feel better about myself because I was making a difference. Instead, my world had been rocked, and I knew I could never go back to the way things were before.*

---

* Thankfully the story doesn't end here. I come back to Honduras in the next chapter with a more hope-filled story.

Back for More

My next step into a bigger understanding of the world came a few years later after I finished college. I decided to leave America for a time and live in Peru to volunteer to teach English as a second language and work as a zookeeper on the side. I wish I could say I moved to Peru because I wanted to keep growing and connecting with people who were different from me. That's not what happened. The move came after a college girlfriend dumped me because she didn't want to date some guy who was on his way to becoming a townie. I believe her exact words were, she didn't want to "get stuck with some guy who could never move beyond Warsaw, Indiana."

My first reaction was, "What's wrong with Warsaw, Indiana?" but I got her point. I loved my hometown, which kept me from seeing how uniform everyone in my little circle actually was. Even when I was in college, most of my friends were exactly like me. Once I was finished at Indiana University, I planned on moving back to my hometown. Honestly, I didn't see any problem with my plans until my girlfriend dumped me. That hit me hard and caused me to take a long look at my life. When I got the chance to move to South America, I took it. I wanted to prove to myself that my ex-girlfriend was wrong about me.

Living in Peru didn't crush my entire world quite like my first mission trip to Honduras. However, the experience changed me. In order to connect with the Peruvian people, I wanted to learn as much about their country and culture as I could. I felt like I needed to see their world the way they saw it. That's when I first learned about the Spanish conquistadors and how they treated the Incan people.

Before I went to Peru, I knew that most of the people there were

Roman Catholic. After I arrived, I learned why. The conquistadors came in and destroyed huge Incan cities and built churches on top of them. The Incans converted to Catholicism, but that's because it was convert or die. This did not fit the picture of Jesus I grew up with. I wondered how I'd feel about Christianity if the Inca story had been my family's history. I'd never thought about my faith like that before. This was my first step into seeing the world through the eyes of those completely different from myself. Something just felt right about doing this.

My understanding changed even more as I began connecting with the odd collection of people who shared the hostel where I lived. People from all over the world came in and out of that house. They ranged in age from their twenties up to their seventies. None of us really had anything in common except for the fact that we were all far from home. That was enough. Meals were my favorite times. Everybody in the house would sit down to eat together, which led to us talking and connecting with one another. We all talked about our different beliefs and the different ways we saw the world, but no one argued. In fact, everybody seemed genuinely interested in getting to know one another. The fact that all of us were so far from the familiar brought us together. Being strangers in a far-off country was our bridge.

The relationships weren't always easy. These conversations constantly pushed me out of my comfort zone. I had to think through my faith and my nationality and the way I had always thought about the world. It wasn't that people were challenging me in an argumentative way. Instead, these conversations helped me see things through different eyes. The view was like nothing I'd ever seen before. Once again, my small-town, Midwestern-boy bubble was being burst.

Villa de la Vina

Determined not to fall right back into my bubble after my time in Peru, I moved to Denver, Colorado, rather than going back to Indiana. But I discovered bubbles aren't unique to the Midwest, and I might well have slipped back into one despite my good intentions if not for one of my new coworkers. She heard that a reality dating show was looking for contestants and insisted I'd be perfect for it. Long story short, that's how I ended up on *The Bachelorette*. From the moment I climbed into the limo for the ride to the Bachelor mansion, I felt as completely out of my element as I did when our mission team bus pulled into the Honduran village years earlier.

Four other guys got into the car with me, and all four could not have been more different from me, at least from my perspective. They were all better-looking and more successful and more confident. I did not belong in the same car. My sense of inferiority grew even worse when I arrived at the Bachelor mansion and met the rest of the contestants. I could not have been further outside of my comfort zone. These guys were nothing like the guys I hung out with back in Indiana. Thankfully, I was pretty certain I wasn't going to have to be uncomfortable for long. I figured I'd be back in the limo for the ride back to the hotel as soon as the first rose ceremony rolled around and I got sent home.

Except I did not get sent home, and I'm glad I didn't. If I had, I would have missed out on the chance to connect with these other guys as we lived together for several weeks during the filming of the show. The contestants, the other bachelors, came from a wide variety of backgrounds and held a lot of different worldviews. Since we didn't have our own private rooms, I didn't have a safe place to go and hide. I couldn't run back to my old group of friends or get back to my safe little Midwestern Christian bubble. We were all thrown together, 24-7, in a six-bedroom house with a lot of time on our hands. Of course, all of us were vying to win the heart of the Bachelorette, but the dates and the other stuff they show on television still left us with a lot of down time.

Honestly, being on that show proved to be a turning point in my life. With so much time on our hands, the other guys and I talked, listened, and got to know one another on a deep level. I built friendships in that house that continue to this day. Every morning when I got up, I felt like, once again, I'd been kicked out of my comfort zone, but I needed to be. The process of connecting with them was nerve-racking, and it shattered a lot of my belief systems. Yet when my time on the show eventually ended, I went home different in a good way.

I hope at this point you see the trend. Each one of these experiences compounded on the previous one to teach me something new, to once and for all burst my safe little bubble.

Soapbox

For most of my life, I didn't see the bubble I grew up in as a bad thing. I had friends. I connected with other people in a meaningful way. That seemed to be enough. If I'd picked up a book like this and read through this section on community, I'd have said I was already living a very, very connected life.

But I wasn't, and there's a good chance you are not either, because all of us naturally gravitate toward bubbles. There's an old saying,

"Birds of a feather flock together," and it's true. If we walk into a room filled with people we don't know and are forced to interact with them, by the end of the night we will most likely find ourselves grouped together with people just like us. We will find the guy who grew up in a small town or the girl from the Midwest. If we are together with this newfound friend long enough, we might even make a strong connection and build a friendship that lasts the rest of our lives. I'm not saying that's intrinsically "bad," but if we stop there, we stop short of discovering a richness that can never be found in a bubble.

As I look back over my life, I have come to the conclusion that I need to constantly make a conscious effort to break out of my bubble. Breaking out means more than visiting a different country or talking with people unlike ourselves. We need to connect with those who see the world in a completely different way than we do. You and I need to spend significant time with friends who were raised in a different culture with a different set of assumed beliefs. Yes, venturing outside our comfort zones is scary and uncomfortable and can rock our worlds, but that's the only way to see a full and complete picture of our world. You can never see the world in the truest way through the prism of a bubble. However, connections with those truly different from us don't just happen. They take a lot of work on our part.

When I think about connecting with people who are outside my bubble, I always find myself going back to my experience on that first mission trip to Honduras. Before I left, I was scared. I genuinely was. You don't have to travel to a third-world country to experience fear of connection. I think it hits everyone. You hear it in the way one tribe talks about another tribe. We use words like *us* and *them*, and those we deem *them* are always a scary bunch. Most groups have stereotypes for those who aren't like us, which lets us prejudge and assume things about people without going to the trouble of getting to know them. We don't have to get to know them to be afraid of what they might do to us or our way of life. I hear all this, and I wonder—what are we really afraid of? Are we afraid that if we genuinely listen to those who see the world in a different way, we might discover our beliefs are wrong? But, at the end of this whole thing, are we not all looking to pursue truth in all things, in all ways? So what good is it to hide from different perspectives and sets of experiences?

Connecting with others can also be difficult because we have a tendency either to look down on those who are different as somehow inferior, or to look up at them with jealousy. When I first went to Honduras and saw the conditions in which these villagers lived, I did look down on them, as if they had somehow chosen to live in such poverty. Many years and many, many trips back to Honduras later (which I'll talk more about in the next chapter), I find myself in awe of these same people because of their strength and resiliency and authenticity. I could not connect with them on that first trip because I was too busy feeling sorry for them to look across and see them as the same as me. The same was true in my limo ride to the Bachelor mansion. I found myself so intimidated by these guys that I couldn't connect. When we feel intimidated by others, we usually feel jealous of what they have as well. It's hard to connect with someone when you secretly wish they would get knocked down a peg or two. I had to get over those feelings before I could open up and have honest conversations with them.

I say all of this not to simply tell you my story. I am telling you this because most of us are blind to the ideological bubbles in which we hide. We live in the most isolated time in history, and as everyone who has lived through the COVID-19 isolation orders knows all too well, isolation takes its toll. Living safely locked inside an ideological bubble, completely separated from anyone who looks different or thinks differently or sees the world through a different lens, is just as damaging as being stuck inside your house indefinitely. I don't know about you, but I couldn't wait for the all clear to sound so that I could get out and go hang with my friends or go to church and worship in person rather than watching services on a computer screen. The months of isolation reminded us that we are made to connect with others, which is why we have to break out and make meaningful connections beyond our safe little bubbles.

In the last book of the Bible, in a picture of heaven painted in Revelation 7:9, the writer described "a great multitude that no one could count, from every nation, tribe, people and language, standing before the throne and before the Lamb" (NIV). On that day, race won't matter and culture won't matter and money won't matter—nothing that divides us now will matter. Instead, we will all be united, singing praises to the One who loves us more than our minds can understand. I believe what will be true someday in heaven can be true here on earth—all it takes is for each one of us to break out of our bubbles and take that scary trip into our discomfort zone to connect. The trip is worth it, and the bubble is worth bursting!

CHAPTER 9

An Entry Point to Do Good

One year after my first mission trip, I returned to the same Honduran villages. I still wasn't over what I felt the first time, but I hoped that maybe things had improved. One of my friends, Riley, came along on the second trip. The two of us knew one another through our church. He was supposed to come on the trip with his parents my first year, but he skipped it and then wrecked his dad's car while his parents were gone. They didn't give him a choice the next year, which is how he ended up going to Honduras with me. My expectations had changed by the second trip. Receiving my neon T-shirt didn't thrill me like it did the year before. Nor did I think of the trip as walking into battle. The members of our team didn't face anything compared to what the people in the villages lived with every day.

When we got off the bus, I saw that nothing had changed. The shacks, the children with their sores and stick-thin arms and legs, everything was pretty much exactly the way it was the year before. I looked over at Riley, and he was clearly shaken. He kept staring at one house in particular. A tarp covered the top of the house and came down over the sides. Printed across the tarp in big, black letters were the words, "Delta Trash." Riley's neck and ears turned red like he was about to explode.

"Do you see that, Ben?" he asked me.

"Yeah," I said.

"Their house . . . it tells them they're trash." His voice cracked, he was so angry.

"I know," I said, shaking my head.

"Why'd we get so lucky to win the birth lottery?" Riley asked with disgust.

"I don't know, man, I don't know," I said. Now Riley knew why I'd been so angry for the past year.

"We've got to do something," Riley said. "This just isn't right."

I agreed we or someone needed to do something, but I didn't know what that could be. Riley and I were basically just kids. Riley was five years older than me, but I was in high school and Riley was in his early twenties. How could two kids actually make a difference in a village where the people had very little food, no clean water, and no education opportunities beyond maybe a sixth-grade level? The area around them had an enormously high crime rate, and most of these people lived on maybe two dollars a day. In our minds, the issues seemed too complex for us to tackle. We couldn't fix them, and even if we could do something, how would we even know where to start? That's why the situation made me so angry. I could see something had to be done, but I felt powerless to do anything beyond our annual trip to pass out some food and used clothes. That effort seemed almost useless, but at least it was something.

But there was something else that ate at me. As well-intentioned as our mission trips to Honduras were, there remained a huge disconnect between us and the people we went to serve. Sure, we engaged them in conversations as best we could and did our best to show them genuine love, but the trip still felt like we had come down to save, not serve. Our time with the people in the village was limited. None of us really spoke the language fluently, and none of us could relate to the day-to-day lives of the villagers. On top of that, we never took the time to really listen to the people in the villages. Instead, we came down with an agenda that *we* felt met some of their most pressing needs, swooped in for a few hours, did our thing, and left.

Connecting in a meaningful and genuine way went beyond the scope of what we could do in one of these short-term trips. I came away wishing we could do more than just a swoop-in visit but, again, I had no idea how to do that.

Something More

Riley and I went home and got on with our regularly scheduled lives. I kept thinking about the people in the villages we had visited, but the more I thought about it, the angrier and more frustrated I became. Honestly, I was angry with God. How did God, in his wisdom, think it was fair for me to live in such ease while the people in the village suffer every day based solely on where they were born?

Then one day Riley called me. "Are you still angry about what we saw in Honduras?" he asked.

"Yeah," I said. "That's been bugging me for a long time."

"I think I have a solution," Riley said. "What if we go back to the same villages, but instead of handing stuff out and then leaving, we start by asking them what they need, what they want, and what they dream of?" he asked. "What if instead of pushing our agenda as if we know what is best for them, we really got to know people and partnered with them to help them get to where they want to be? What if our whole purpose of going down to their homes was to help build a sustainable future for their next generations?"

"I think that's a great idea," I said.

That conversation led to many more conversations, which eventually led to Riley launching a nonprofit called Humanity and Hope. I could write an entire book on Humanity and Hope because I am all-in on its purpose and mission. I've served on the board since its start, and I've traveled with Riley to Honduras more times than I can count. Out of the connections and conversations with people in villages across Honduras, H&H invests its time and resources into what H&H calls the Six Pillars:

1. Infrastructure (shelter and clean water)
2. Economy (through developing income-producing opportunities)
3. Community
4. Health
5. Education
6. Leadership development

None of these are quick fixes—they all require a long-term commitment and working alongside our partners in Honduras. This isn't work we do *for* them but *with* them. The payoff comes in conversations like the one I had with a friend in Honduras about a year after H&H installed our first clean-water system in a Honduran village. During a hot, sunny day in a community outside of San Pedro Sula, I asked my friend, a thirty-five-year-old woman, what it had been like for the past year. She smiled, stared into my eyes, and said, "I woke up without a stomachache for the first time in my life."

Stories like those of my friends in Honduras are a key part of why I have written this book. The point of the past four chapters is to encourage you to connect with others. But there's more to connecting with people than building a relationship with them. I constantly ask myself what I want to accomplish with this brief life I've been given. Like you, I want my life to matter. I would like to think that at the end of my life I will have made a difference in the lives of others. I mean, who knows, possibly one day when I have come and gone, there may be a great-grandchild that hears my name mentioned and says, "Wow, I wish I would have known great-grandpa Ben." Most people I meet say the same thing. We all want to do great things with our lives. No one wants to get to the end and look back and realize our time on earth was wasted.

And that's why we must connect with others. We can do more together than we ever could do on our own. Now, if you were born without the desire to do great things and would prefer to live in complete isolation and tell a story free of risk and adventure, then this isn't for you. But I think most of us do want our lives to count. That's why we need each other. Together we can do what one person could never do.

Working together to do something that matters is also the best way to connect with other people. I love nothing more than getting together with my friends at a local pub and having a beer and talking or watching a ball game. Those are good times. But I have to say that my strongest relationships are those that grow out of working together to do good, especially when the work is hard and we are pushed to our limits to try to do it. That kind of pressure pushes people together and creates a stronger and faster connection than a thousand nights of watching ballgames ever could.

This idea is more than just a chapter in a book for me. I can honestly say that this is what I've done my best to focus my life on. A few years ago it hit me that the best thing I could do with my life is find a way to connect people to do good together. And the genesis of the idea for how to do that came to me in—where else?—Honduras.

The Generous Story

In July 2017 Riley and I returned to Honduras, but instead of working, we decided to travel all around the country to see parts of it we'd never seen before. We wanted to see the capital beyond the airport as well as the other main cities. It's a beautiful country, and we really just wanted to get to know it.

The idea for the trip came after Riley met a man who owned one of the largest exporting companies in the country. The man invited Riley to come down and hang out at his coffee farm. We both loved coffee, but we'd never seen where it came from beyond a bag in the store. The funny thing was, once we actually got to the country and walked around the first coffee farm either one of us had ever visited, both Riley and I were struck with a sense that there had to be some bigger reason for us being there. Neither of us knew what that might be or even if our sense was right. The feeling might have been nothing more than a carryover of the weight we felt on every other trip we'd made with Humanity and Hope. Those trips always had a larger vision and purpose. It felt strange to be in Honduras with nothing more on our agenda than riding four-wheelers and seeing a coffee bush for the first time. I didn't even know coffee grows on a bush or that coffee beans are actually berries. Maybe discovering these odd facts was the reason we were there. Neither of us really knew.

A few days into our trip, I began to feel overwhelmed by what we were learning. I was struck by how intricate the process of delivering the coffee bean to my coffee cup really was. We saw literally hundreds of people picking the coffee beans by hand and others walking down a mountain with hundreds of pounds on their backs. I'd read about fair-trade coffee and how so many farmers were paid pennies on the dollar for their harvest, but now I saw with my own eyes what that meant. And what do you know, this little red berry with a coffee bean inside was bursting my bubble of comfort again (I just really like bubbles bursting). Still, though, I wasn't quite sure what I was to do with all the information slapping me in the face. Was this why we were there, to learn more about why fair-trade coffee is so vital? I still had no idea.

The picture started to come into focus one night when Riley and I met a friend for dinner. It was one of those magical nights, the kind I will never forget. We ate outside under the light of the stars. Wine and food flowed, and the more we drank and ate, the deeper our conversations went (weird how that happens, huh?). Our friend started asking about Humanity and Hope, and Riley and I told him about the new communities we planned to enter and how we were in the process of trying to build a school. Basically, we talked about everything you'd expect two guys involved in a community-development nonprofit to talk about. At one point in the conversation, one of us added something like, "We have so much planned that it's going to be hard to raise enough money to make it all happen, but we think we can do it."

Our friend replied, "What is your fundraising strategy?"

Riley and I looked at one another. We really didn't have any kind of strategy beyond talking up Humanity and Hope around our friends and on social media, hoping someone wanted to donate.

"What happens if that doesn't work out?" our friend asked. When we didn't answer right away, he continued, "If your fundraising work falls apart, or if either of the two of you can't devote the same amount of time and energy to it that you are now, what happens to the communities where you are now working? I'll tell you what will happen. They'll be worse off than they would have been if you'd never shown up. Right now, they have jobs and schools because of your partnership. But if that partnership ever ends, they're sunk."

"But we aren't going to just leave," I said.

"You can say that, but life happens and unexpected things hit. Then what? What you need is a sustainable model to fund the organization, which will allow you to commit to being in the communities for a very long time."

That sounded like a great idea in theory.

"So what would something like that look like?" Riley asked.

"You can find one big donor, an individual or a corporate donor, and have them donate enough money that you can operate off of the interest every year. Or, you can start a for-profit company and donate your profits back into the nonprofit. If the company grows, the work here will grow, which keeps you from having to hope that Aunt Sally gives the same thousand dollars this year that she gave last," our friend said.

The conversation swirled in my head as Riley and I headed off to our room that night. Lying in the dark on opposite sides of the room, we started talking about the challenge we faced. The work with Humanity and Hope was growing every year, but how could we sustain it? We'd never thought about that before. We both were still young enough that we assumed what had worked in the past would work in the future. The longer we talked, the more I started thinking about what I needed to do with this. At that point in time I still worked for the same software company where I worked before my turn in the reality-television spotlight. Most weeks I put in my time at the company, then flew off to Los Angeles or wherever for press tours and meet-and-greets with fans of the show. It was like I lived two lives. In one I wrote software manuals. In the other I walked red carpets while cameras flashed and people shouted my name. Then it was back to Denver and back to my cubicle. The dichotomy was confusing for me personally. I was ready for a change.

And for the first time in years, change looked possible. Prior to this trip, as most twentysomethings do, I had started to imagine what my life might look like if I stepped away from software sales. I had been offered a couple of commercial partnerships connected to my podcast, so a change was more than wishful thinking. This was the first time it felt realistic to let my mind wander to a place of actually walking away. And if I stepped away from my day job, and could be supported by the commercial tie-ins, that might free up time to do something even bigger.

"If we started something, I am about to be in a position where I could devote my time to it without having to receive a salary from it,"

I said. That led to more talks about what kind of company we could start, which took us right back to the coffee fields we'd visited over the past several days. Around the world, coffee is more than a beverage. It brings people together and tells a story. That's what we wanted to do with our company. Connection over shared experiences was at the core. And coffee felt like a catalyst for connection. We started dreaming about a company that not only would generate profits that could finance the work of Humanity and Hope but could also bring people together as an entry point to do good.

By the time we got up the next morning, we had already decided to go forward and start the process of creating a new company as soon as we returned home to the States. I won't overwhelm you with all the stories of how we got our company off the ground. Basically, it was a lot of work. We had to build relationships with businesses to make this dream of a fair-trade coffee company, which was more than a coffee company, a reality. Eventually we partnered with a roasting company in Fort Wayne, Indiana, that shared a similar vision. Over time we also put together the infrastructure we'd need. Riley had a business degree, which helped work out a lot of the details. Another friend, Drew Scholl, joined us, and the three of us cofounded the company. We just didn't have a name for it yet.

A name is crucial in an enterprise like this, so we hired a marketing company to come up with one for us. They came back with "Ben's Beans." That was definitely not a name we could use. For one thing, I couldn't see anyone sitting down in the morning and pouring themselves a cup of "Ben's Beans." For another, the last thing I wanted to do was put my name front and center, as if this company and its mission were all about me. I'd already done a trip for the pats on the back, and the experience rang very hollow. I wasn't about to do it again.

Riley, Drew, and I were stuck when it came to a name. The three of us were back in Indiana at my parents' house on the lake when we started talking about where we were with the company and where we hoped to go. My mom sat back, listening to our conversation. Finally, she said, "Well it sounds like what you three boys are doing is very generous." Riley, Drew, and I looked at one another and said, "That's it. That's the name: Generous."

But the name and the mission and the company weren't all we created. From the start we built into Generous an ambassador program, which I mentioned in Brandon's story in chapter 3. Since we started this company as a way of funding a bigger mission, it only seemed natural to invite people to come and join us to do good not only in Honduras but wherever people are. Generous is all about connecting people, and the ambassador program gives us a reason to come together. It's a way of making a difference together. A shared purpose and a shared passion based on something healthy and good leads us to do more together than we could ever do by ourselves. This is the antidote to the most isolated time in our history. We need to break out of our silos and connect with something bigger than ourselves.

Reality

Before we continue on, I need to give one disclaimer. Talking about connecting with other people and making a difference in the world can feel like a big pep rally speech. We all get excited, and we go off with this picture in our mind of how great this is going to be and how the work won't feel like work but instead we'll all feel really good about ourselves. That's not exactly how this works. Don't get me wrong. I love my work with Generous. At the time of this writing, I'm coming up on three years with the company, and in those three years we've seen more growth than we ever dreamed possible. Most days I wake up pumped that I get to be a part of this work.

But it is work.

Some days it feels like a lot of work, much like a typical job. Many of my weekends are still filled with red carpet events where I put on a suit and look my best and cameras show up and snap pictures and reporters shout out questions while fans call my name. And then I jump on a plane and head back home, because I have to be up before six the next morning to drag tables into a convention center where I will serve coffee all day to promote the work of Generous. Twenty-four hours earlier I was on the red carpet at the American Music Awards. The next day I'm in a T-shirt and jeans, cleaning out machines and grinding beans and brewing coffee and smiling until my face hurts and making small talk as I pour. No one shouts out my name, and no one wants my autograph. Instead, I'm hustling coffee. The glitz and glamour and all the attention can feel really good, but the work is what matters.

This is why we connect. Not to feel good about ourselves but to make a difference. That's what pulls me out of my silos and breaks me out of my bubble. Connecting with others to do something so much bigger than myself that my mind can't really take it all in—that's what makes a life worth living.

Reconnected Romantically

CHAPTER 10

True Love

What is romantic love? Some of us skip through life, assuming we know the answer. We know love when we *feel* love. But how do we know what we feel is actually love? Could it be nothing more than primal instinct and lust? At first the two feel a lot alike. We meet someone and sense an instantaneous attraction. Sparks fly. Hearts flutter. Blood flows. The moment we first speak to one another we feel the chemistry. Then our hands touch and it's (to borrow a line from an old movie) *magic*. When our lips meet for the first time, fireworks explode.

But are fireworks proof of true romantic love? Sparks may fly, but are sparks enough for us to know this is the *one* we will be with forever? Chemistry doesn't equal a healthy relationship, something many of us have learned the hard way. Nor do the feelings of being *in love* mean we've found our one true love. Again, I must ask, what is true romantic love?

I have wanted to pursue true love for as long as I can remember. My parents started praying for my future partner even before I was born. Anything they'd pray about for so long must be a big, Big, BIG deal. Anything this big had to be taken seriously, and I didn't want to blow it. That's why one day, while laying shingles and pounding nails on my roof with my dad, I asked him, "Dad, how did you know Mom was the one?" At the time my mom and dad had been together for thirty-seven years. The two of them still seemed madly in love. If ever I have witnessed true love, it has to be my mom and dad's relationship. I wanted to know their secret.

I sat back and waited for my dad to let me in on the secret that unlocks the mystery of finding true love. I honestly expected him to say something life changing, to give me some profound truth that would illuminate my path toward true love. My dad paused for a few moments as he thought about my question, then said, "Ben, when you know, you know."

And that, my dear readers, is the David Higgins secret to understanding true love! *When you know, you know.*

I could not hide my surprise. My jaw dropped in shock and I asked, "Is that all you've got?"

"Yep, that's it," my dad said with a smile like he actually had revealed one of the great mysteries of the universe. "When you know, you know," he said again.

I shook my head. "I don't get it," I said. "When you know, you know? That makes no sense to me. How am I ever supposed to *know*? What does that even mean?"

My dad grinned and shrugged his shoulders. "You'll just know," he said again.

Except, for most of my life, I haven't even known what I was supposed to know. I've felt sparks. I've seen fireworks. I've felt the euphoria where I'd gladly drive four hours on a Tuesday night just to spend a couple of hours with the one I love, then drive back home in the middle of the night and get up tired for work the next day, and then do it again on Wednesday if that's what it took to see her again. But the euphoria didn't last and neither did the relationship. None of my relationships did for the first thirty years of my life.

At My Worst

That conversation on the roof with my dad was fresh in my mind when I agreed to be the Bachelor. A friend recently asked me what I hoped to find when I went on the show. When I flew to Los Angeles to start shooting, I guess I thought I was off to find true love, even though I wasn't exactly sure what that meant. Before I first appeared on *The Bachelorette*, it had been at least a year, maybe more, since I had pursued any kind of romantic connection. Between living in South America and then moving to a city where I literally knew no one, I didn't have a lot of opportunities to find someone special. After a while, not pursuing a romantic connection became easier than looking for one. I'd had so little success in the dating world that I'd pretty much stopped putting myself out there even before I moved to Denver. Living single felt safer, with less shame and guilt. This may be a very clever excuse, but I also felt like it was easier to follow God's lead without any sort of romantic connections to get in the way. Even so, when the chance to go on *The Bachelorette* came three years after moving to

Denver, I took it. And when ABC approached me about becoming the Bachelor after that, I also said yes. Why? What was I really looking for in my search for love?

The longer I thought about my friend's question, the more it brought me back to the question I asked earlier: What is romantic love? When I think about the relationships I've pursued, not just romantically but with my friends as well, I think all relationships flow out of one universal desire. When everything else is stripped away, I believe we all hope to find someone who will see the real us and still love us. By *real me* I mean me on my worst days, when everything goes wrong and my patience runs out. I mean the me I can hardly admit lives inside of me who comes boiling up to the surface. Yes, I want to find "the one" who will make my heart skip a beat, the one who makes me want to be the best version of myself. Yet what I really want to find is the one who makes me want to be a better me but will still love me with the same intensity when the worst me comes out.

But there's more to loving me at my worst than loving me when I'm tired and cranky. I'm talking about my real worst. I'm talking about finding someone who will love me when they hear the stories of my past, stories I never want to share but realize I have to if I am ever going to completely open myself up to this other person. More than anything I've always wanted to find someone who sees and understands all of who I am and can still love me.

But it's not just about me. To be loved like this means I have to reciprocate this love with the same intensity in the same circumstances. If I ever hope to find someone who will love me at my worst, I have to be joyfully willing to do the same. And that's what makes this all so hard. Longing to be loved when we are at our worst is easy;

choosing to joyfully and passionately love another on their worst day is where real love begins.

Naked and Unashamed

When I consider what it means to love another at both their best and their worst, I find myself going back to my favorite picture of romantic love, which is found in the second chapter of the Bible. Genesis 2:25 says, "Now the man and his wife were both naked, but they felt no shame." Naked and unashamed speaks of far more than the fact that they did not yet feel the need for clothing. The first two people still lived in a state of innocence that some Bible scholars compare to the innocence of a young child who has no sense of shame when they dart through the house without any clothes on. But Adam and Eve were not young children, and the words *naked* and *unashamed* speak to more than a lack of self-consciousness. The phrase comes immediately after the verse which says, "This explains why a man leaves his father and mother and is joined to his wife, and the two are united into one" (Genesis 2:24). The two became one and stood before each other naked and unashamed. That is, the two stood before one another with nothing to hide physically, emotionally, or spiritually. They were completely open, absolutely vulnerable, without fear of rejection, and without shame. Isn't that what we really hope to find when we search for true love?

The phrase "naked and unashamed" isn't something most people use every day to define romantic love. Instead we use words like *acceptance* and *comfort* and *support*. The idea is the same. Naked and unashamed means laying oneself completely bare before another person and telling them that you want to go through life together because you believe that the two of you will be better than either of you would be alone. You don't simply fall into love this deep.

I think that's what my dad meant by saying, "When you know, you know." There comes a point where you *know* this is the person you can open up to fully without fear or shame. You instinctively realize you can choose to take off your mask and choose not to be shocked when I take off mine. I choose to let you see the real me, and I choose to love and accept the real you. This is true romantic love, where both partners stay consistent in their joyful decision to participate in the acceptance of the other.

Love as a choice doesn't sound very romantic, I get that, but true love demands it. Standing naked and unashamed today doesn't come nearly as easy to us as it did to Adam and Eve. The first man and woman didn't have pasts they had to deal with. They didn't bring along emotional baggage from previous relationships. Nor did they have scars, either physical or emotional, that they'd rather keep hidden. Neither had a past of suffering abuse, nor did either have to work through complicated parental relationships that made it hard for them to fully trust another human. They hadn't been let down by people they trusted or blindsided by someone's unfaithfulness. None of the things that make relationships really complicated today had happened to them yet, which made this level of openness much easier for them than it is for us.

However, the first man and woman also had some disadvantages. Neither had ever seen a successful relationship in action. They didn't have a strong relationship between their own parents or peers' parents to look to as an example of what it takes to make love last. The two really didn't have a clue about each other. They'd been thrown together. Neither had a chance to get to know the other over time in relaxed, nonromantic settings. Given the situation, I would expect one or both to be completely guarded with the other until the other proved they could be trusted with this level of intimacy.

But that's not how the story goes. Adam and Eve were naked and unashamed, completely open, completely vulnerable.

Naked, unashamed, completely open, vulnerable. When I reflect on these words, they speak to me of the process by which we tear down all the walls we have put up to protect our hearts from being hurt and pull off all the masks we hide behind. I picture someone coming down the hall to their spouse, slowly taking off their hat and their gloves and their shirt, exposing more and more vulnerability with each step. Instead of literal clothes, I see this as emotionally stripping off the shame we bring into relationships, along with the guilt and confusion of our past failures. It's showing the scars, the wounds, the lumps and bruises, the battle wounds of life. Every point of vulnerability is laid bare, along with the pride and pretense we use to keep others at arm's length. All of it comes down as we open ourselves up completely without shame or fear or embarrassment.

The Amplified Bible translates Genesis 2:25 as, "And the man and his wife were both naked and were not ashamed *or* embarrassed" (emphasis added). That's the idea. No shame. No embarrassment. It's saying, "This is who I really am," without fear of rejection. It's being completely and fully accepted with an openness to learn and discover more about each other. For me, I see this as a kind of holy imagination at play, one where this connection says that it doesn't know where this relationship will ultimately lead, but that's okay. The two become one, which means that they're both open to whatever the future may hold together.

Obviously, this kind of romantic connection does not occur instantaneously. The root of it may sprout in an instant and may even throw up initial sparks, but its depth demands it grow slowly and steadily over time. I've heard couples who have been together forever speak of it in terms of being more in love after forty years of marriage than they were the day they said "I do." I am certain that "naked and unashamed" gets to the heart of romantic connections that last. The openness and vulnerability grow so much stronger over time and become more and more of a beautiful thing. I believe this is what we desire when we talk about romantic love. We don't just want to wake up beside someone who will love us unconditionally today. We want to wake up beside them every day for the rest of our lives.

I believe every human heart craves the intimacy described in Genesis 2:25. Yet I also believe it is impossible for us to connect on a "naked and unashamed" level if we do not already possess this sort of connection within ourselves. That is, not only *can* you be romantically connected as a single person, I believe you *must* be before you can ever connect romantically with another person. Even if we never connect romantically with another person, either by choice or not, we need to be able to stand before ourselves naked and unashamed. You and I need to be able to look at ourselves and see ourselves as worthy and deserving of love because we *are* worthy and deserving of love. No other person can fully give us this level of validation, not until we already have it inside ourselves. My friend Tanya figured this out in a more complete and powerful way than anyone I know. Hers is a story we all need to hear.

CHAPTER 11

Single, Not Sad

W hen you think of people in a romantic relationship, what is the first picture that pops in your head? I'll give you a minute. Here's mine: a couple walking down the beach, holding hands, smiling. I think of candlelight and soft music, gentle kisses, and long talks about anything and everything. Songwriters have extolled the wonder of love. There's even a book of the Bible that's devoted completely to the wonder of romantic love, which starts with the words, "Kiss me and kiss me again, for your love is sweeter than wine" (Song of Songs 1:2). That's what most of us picture when we think of people in a romantic relationship. Love. Joy. Passion. The deepest longing of our hearts fulfilled.

Now, what is the picture that pops in your head when you think of someone who is single? By single I don't just mean unmarried. I mean someone who is not romantically connected to anyone in any formal way. For a guy, we usually think of someone on a couch, sitting in front of the TV, playing video games late into the night. Or he's out with his friends all the time, hoping to find a girl. When you think of a single girl, the picture is even more bleak. My friend Tanya put it this way: "When you picture single, you picture a girl sitting in front of her TV, eating ice cream."

We may not carry these exact images of what it means to be single, but in my experience, no matter what gender we are speaking of, many people act like singleness is a disease that needs to be cured. When someone discovers you are single, it's not that they look down on you. They just feel sorry for you. An attitude of *Oh, you poor thing*, comes across in both their looks and words. That stands in sharp contrast to the words of the apostle Paul, who wrote, "I wish everyone were single, just as I am. Yet each person has a special gift from God, of one kind or another" (1 Corinthians 7:7). I think this is one of the most radical verses in the Bible I've ever read. According to Paul, singleness is to be celebrated, not pitied. He presents it as a higher calling. And yet the reaction to singleness, especially in church, is so opposite to his words. As I learned after my big breakup, everyone seems to think singles are broken. Tanya put it like this: "I'm single, not sad." She's also one of the most confident, fully together, and encouraging people I've ever been around. That's why I wanted to include her story here.

I met Tanya a few years ago when I walked into the iHeartRadio studios to record my first *Almost Famous* podcast with fellow *Bachelor* alum Ashley Iaconetti. I was nervous and felt out of place. Everything about doing studio work seemed completely foreign to me. Then Tanya came over and introduced herself. I may have been out of place, but this was her world and she did her best to make me feel at home. Even though I was a complete rookie, she didn't treat me like one. We started talking and I couldn't help but notice this warm, bubbly, smart woman exuded a quiet confidence. I admired the way she treated everyone with such respect and how open she was to talk about her life and her faith.

Tanya also happens to be single by choice. "I've been on apps and I've been set up and I'm dating, but I hold a high standard not just for myself but for anyone that I might date. *Picky* isn't the word. I think I'm just a lot more self-aware now." *Now* is the key word in that statement. Tanya has been completely self-aware as long as I've known her, but, as she told me, it's been a journey for her to reach this point in her life.

A Typical Beginning

Through her teens and early twenties, Tanya never stayed single for long. She jumped from relationship to relationship, from guy to guy. Like most of us, she craved real romantic connection. She wanted the passion and the candlelight and the love that grows stronger over time. Dating was fun, but she also had a clear expectation of where she hoped it would take her. Ever since she was little, she wanted to have it all, and to her "all" meant a job she enjoyed, a husband she loved and who loved her, and a family to take care of—all by the age of twenty-five.

Yet, all through this time in her life, Tanya didn't know who she was or what she really wanted. Her anxiety over being alone or going to events by herself kept her in some relationships longer than she probably should have been. Often she found herself conforming to what she thought the guy wanted rather than being herself. She bent over backward and put his needs above her own. At times she gave herself physically before she wanted to, not because she felt pressured, but because she thought if she didn't, he'd lose interest. But physical intimacy never led to the commitment she wanted, leaving her in a perpetual state of pain. She found herself analyzing why this guy she thought might love her was suddenly talking to other women. With her, when she's in, she's all in. Tanya had given everything to this guy. What kept him from giving himself fully to her?

The turning point came when a serious relationship abruptly ended. Before the breakup, Tanya thought this guy was the one, the be-all and end-all. But he wasn't and his leaving shook her to her core. It wasn't just the breakup but also the realization that the grand plan she had for her life, her having it all with the great job and loving husband and family, wasn't going to come true any time soon, if ever. Tanya's world had been flipped upside down. Deflated and defeated, she kept wondering what was wrong with her. She kept asking herself why she couldn't keep a guy. Deep down she longed for romantic connection, to love and be loved, but none of her romantic relationships had lasted. *Why?* she kept asking herself. *What is wrong with me?*

Tanya grew up attending a formal Orthodox church with her parents, but it was not something that she had connected with on a personal level. After this breakup she found herself praying again. Every morning and night she prayed the same prayer over and over: "Dear God, please bring us back together." She even went back to church and began attending a Bible study. But she didn't just attend. This particular church presented God as much more accessible than what she'd experienced growing up. Instead of focusing on ceremony and recited lines, they talked about a God who wanted a relationship with her. She wanted that as well.

The more she pursued that relationship, the more personal her prayers became. Her anxiety over being alone subsided as she started experiencing God's presence. She kept praying, every morning and night, and as she grew in her relationship with God, so did her trust in God's plan for her life. Before, she viewed the breakup as divine punishment for something she must have done wrong. Now she knew God loved her unconditionally and only wanted what was best for her. That realization changed her prayer life. Instead of pleading, "God, bring back my boyfriend," she began asking, "God, show me why. You didn't break up this relationship to cause me pain. You broke it up for a bigger reason. Help me see it. Show me, God, what you want."

"I need help through the process," she started praying.

I don't mean to imply that going to church and praying immediately gave her the confidence and faith she exhibits today. The process took time, lots of time, along with lots of confusion and tears. The transformation started with small adjustments she made day by day in her life. She also decided to stay single for a year rather than jump into another serious relationship. While she still dated, the dates weren't part of a husband interview process.

Through that year she discovered several things about herself. One of the biggest was the realization that she'd wasted far too much time focusing on what she *wasn't* instead of being content with who she was. She'd dated guys who had also dated models and actresses. Tanya had found herself constantly comparing herself to the people these guys used to date. Then it hit her: *I am unique and have so much to offer someone. Why compare myself to anyone else? Because I can never be them and they will never be me.* Once she stopped comparing herself to others, walls tumbled down as her sense of self-worth grew.

The Wait

Another turning point came one day while listening to an Oprah podcast. Oprah interviewed DeVon Franklin and his wife, Meagan Good. Tanya recognized the names, which kept her listening. DeVon and Meagan were talking about their book, *The Wait: A Powerful Practice for Finding the Love of Your Life and the Life You Love*. What they said resonated inside Tanya. She wanted to learn more. As soon as the podcast ended, she ordered the book. That book made some ideas that had floated around in her brain come together. She brought DeVon to the iHeartRadio studios for an interview, which proved to be life changing. It was like he could see right through her. He knew exactly where her pain from her past relationships came from. He saw that she was constantly trying to impress, to fill a role and be a chameleon rather than be fully herself.

As Tanya interviewed DeVon, she thought back to all the times she wondered why guys would not commit to her even as she gave her all to them. From that moment on she made up her mind to take back that part of herself. She knew what she most wanted in a relationship. When I asked her how she defined romantic love, she still spoke of love and passion and candlelight, but she also added something I never forgot. "Real love," she said, "takes time to nurture and develop, like cooking a soufflé." In her past she'd lived in the world of quick gratification, like grabbing a scoop of ice cream. But real love isn't like ice cream. It needs to be nurtured and allowed to grow. Her dessert analogy struck a chord with me. Tanya loves sweets, and so do I.

Years have passed since that life-turning breakup, but Tanya feels God has made her single for this long period of time to show her what she's capable of on her own. Today, she's grown personally and professionally and spiritually into someone she never thought she would be. As she looks at her life and the success God has given her, she knows she never could have done this if she had been in a romantic relationship, especially if she was still the person she was before the breakup and spiritual awakening. Her relationship with God has kept her centered as she realizes she has a much larger relationship with the One who is not fleeting, the One who is with her 24-7 and will not walk out on her. Before, she depended on the guy in her life to fill her every need: emotionally, relationally, even spiritually. Now she has a confidence that grows out of depending upon God. It may sound like a cliché, but it's her story.

Tanya still has a strong desire to find a romantic life partner, and she's confident God will fulfill that for her. While she trusts God to bring the right partner in his timing, she isn't sitting back and waiting for "the one" to come waltzing into her life. She's been on the dating apps. Friends have set her up on dates, and she's met guys she felt a connection with and given them her number. Yet, as she dates, she has a higher standard not just for a potential future partner but also for herself. She's not afraid to go on a lousy date, or even have a good date or two or three with somebody and then realize that this person is not the long-term partner for her. She wishes them well and moves on with life, without shame and without guilt.

And if the guy breaks it off with her first? I love her line for that: "Man's rejection is God's protection." She also refuses to allow past hurts to keep her from opening herself up today. "You have to keep putting yourself out there," she said. Love isn't just going to come walking through the door.

Maintaining Balance

Tanya also finds it odd how many people assume that when you are single you don't have any love in your life. For her, the opposite is true. Between her close friendships and family relations and her coworkers, her life is filled with love. Of course, there's a difference between the love of a friend or family member and romantic love, yet the latter cannot thrive without the former. Healthy, loving relationships create the strength in one's life to risk the hurt that can come with romantic love. The hurts are not as devastating when you understand that you are already fully loved, both by God and by those he has put in your life.

In her early twenties Tanya didn't really know who she was or what she wanted. Now she does. "I never want to lose myself in a relationship again," she told me. To keep that from happening she's built nonnegotiable time for herself into her busy schedule—time she intends to keep even when she has a husband she loves and a family. On Sundays she goes to church. That won't change. And every single day she sets aside an hour for herself. Whether it's a workout or a yoga class or just an hour of meditation and prayer, she coordinates the rest of her schedule with her hour of Tanya time. Some days it comes early in the morning, and others it comes in the evening, but she's found she needs this hour each day to keep herself centered.

At the end of our time together, I asked her what she would say to another single who found herself or himself struggling with singleness and the desire to be romantically connected when that isn't happening for them. "I think we are taught that you're a dime a dozen and nobody ever feels worthy of love or of the things they have dreamed about or the desires of their hearts," she said. "You feel rejected, and rejection is such a powerful thing. It can really mess with people's heads. I've dealt with so much rejection in my life, more than I can even tell you. But I came to realize that rejection is not about me. When you can do that and stop taking rejection personally, it changes your life for the better. I've always said man's rejection is God's protection, and that's how you have to see everything, to make that change in your perspective. Once you do, you can start healing from the 'He doesn't like me, I'm not enough' mentality and graduate to 'He's just not my guy. Next.' I'm living proof that this works."

I asked her how she deals with the people who see singleness as a disease, those who constantly try to encourage you by saying, "Oh, you'll find somebody."

"I'm truly single by choice at the moment, because I have such a high standard for the partner I want to do life with," she said. She knows she can't change the minds of those who think if you're single, then something must be wrong with you. "I've come to peace with that," she said. "I can't ever change what anybody else thinks. All I can do is just live my life. I feel that right now, I'm really, really happy. I'm thriving. I hope you can see that.

"I'm not always going to be single, but I also think that when I do have a partner, I'm going to live my relationship in a very different way than I would have had I married somebody in my twenties. I want someone who's going to add value to my life. I think that's a big perspective shift for a lot of people. I have a lot of friends who are monkey branchers, and they swing from guy to guy. They just want somebody. I think at the end of the day, that's not conducive to growing, and I constantly want to be growing and pushing myself and my partner."

You may find it odd that I included the story of one of my single friends in a chapter on reconnecting romantically. For me it makes perfect sense. Romantic love can't be found as a result of a desperate search for love and acceptance. Looking to another person to fill the hurts in your life will only leave you disappointed. Reconnecting romantically begins by reconnecting with yourself, taking the power back over your own existence, and living a full and happy life—whether you have someone special to share it with or not. A healthy connection with one's self allows you to make a healthy romantic connection that can stand the test of time. What makes that connection last? I went searching for that answer next.

CHAPTER 12

What Makes Love Last?

Every day Sally told Maurice she loved him, but he never reciprocated. Most days he hardly acknowledged her presence, but Sally kept right on. Day after day she went out of her way to see him, and day after day Maurice barely noticed. From time to time Sally would bring him a little gift, never anything big, just something to show him she loved him. The only gift Maurice ever gave Sally was a small smile, or the gift of his attention, however brief it might be.

Yet Sally's love never faded. It didn't matter to her that a stroke had taken away most of the man she married more than fifty years earlier. He couldn't speak, and he had lost all use of his left side. A feeding tube kept Maurice alive, along with the round-the-clock care he received in the nursing home. But to Sally, the man she loved was still inside the body trapped in the hospital bed, and she was determined to keep on loving him. She had no other choice. Long before in a church in southwestern Oklahoma, she made a promise to Maurice as he did to her. Both pledged to love one another and to remain faithful in good times and bad, in prosperity and adversity, in sickness and in health. One world war, three children, and two strokes later, nothing had changed. Sally kept her promise and continued to love her husband even though she wasn't always sure he knew who she was.

Don't think for a moment it was easy for her. Immediately after Maurice's stroke, all their friends regularly visited the two of them in the Sequoia View Hospital ICU. Sally never left Maurice's side. Once or twice she broke down, wondering if he would ever come home, unsure if she had the strength to keep on going. Somehow she found the strength, even after most people stopped dropping by, even after it became very clear he would never leave a nursing home. Sally did find a way to bring her husband home. Stubborn to a fault, she refused to accept anything as impossible. With her daughter, Mary, a heart specialist from Southern California, at her side, she convinced the doctors to let Maurice come home for a birthday celebration. It was his last trip anywhere.

From that point forward Sally had to content herself with visits at the nursing home. Although Maurice lost all ability to communicate, she never acted like his body was a hollow shell her beloved had already departed from. Every day she would read him the mail and bring him up to date on everything happening in their small California mountain town. In the spring and fall she would badger the nurses to place Maurice in a wheelchair so she could take him outside. There, under a eucalyptus tree, she would sit beside him, holding his hand, reading him the newspaper—two old lovers enjoying one another.[8]

This picture is a heavy one to process, yet these are the moments when life suddenly, or sometimes slowly, starts to feel incredibly real. They shock us into awareness. However, even within the heaviness, this is a picture of true love. This is what romance means. This is what happily ever after looks like. And this is what I want.

Life wasn't easy for Sally and Maurice. He went to war and she stayed behind, wondering if he'd survive. When he came back, they started a family and went through all the ups and downs that brings. Then their "golden years" together were taken away by not one but two strokes. But none of that could stop their love. It outlasted everything, even to the end. When I first read this story, I loved it. But I also asked myself how these two could make their relationship work for so long through everything they'd been through. The answer, I'm told, really isn't that complicated.

Connecting Through Commitment

I'm not any kind of expert on making a romantic connection last a lifetime, which is why I ask a lot of questions. When I first started thinking about this section of this book, I went out and talked to a lot of people. I spoke with a couple who have been married for sixty years, another who've been married for forty, and another who have been married for fifteen. I asked all of them the secret to building and maintaining a relationship that brings joy and fulfillment to both of them. I didn't just want to know how they'd stayed out of divorce court. I wanted to know how they made their relationship work in such a way that they felt more in love today than they did when they first committed to one another.

Every couple gave me the same answer: it all comes down to commitment. They all told me that success comes down to a choice you make every day, an action you take. "Ben," they all said, "when both of you wake up in the morning and you reach across the bed or you look across the breakfast table, you say to one another even without using words, *I choose you not just for today but for tomorrow and for every day after that.* Then you get up the next day and make the same purposeful yet joy-filled decision."

Here's the key to why this works: the couples told me that some days this is a choice, but other days it isn't. Some days you feel it, and some days you don't. There will be days when you don't even really like the person you have chosen to love, and you don't want to be around them right at that moment. But guess what? There are days when they feel the same way about you.

But when you get up every day and make the conscious decision, *I choose you*, you figure out a way to work through whatever has come between you. You choose to work through it because you've both committed yourselves to this partnership for life. And in that choice, in that commitment, that's where the best version of yourself and your greatest happiness lie.

Obviously, this formula will not work if only one person is committed to it. Nor will it work if abuse and infidelity invade the relationship and destroy the foundation of trust that every relationship must have to work. However, when both parties are committed and faithful, and both choose to remain that way every day, the result is a lifelong connection that stands the test of time.

I have to admit that as much as I like the idea of having someone choose me through all the good and bad times, this idea of choosing someone daily even when I'm not feeling it can seem a bit restrictive. Why would anyone want to wake up next to someone they may not like every day? I wonder if there might be a better way, or at least a more lenient option. When I asked the couples this question, they just smiled at me and shook their heads. There is no other way, at least none that they have found. This kind of unconditional, all-in-no-matter-what commitment is what they've built their lives together on.

Better to Give

As I listen to one couple after another tell me the same thing, the idea of choosing to love brings to mind another word: *sacrifice*. That's really what they're talking about. *Sacrifice* means I set aside my own freedoms and self-interests for my partner. No longer do I look across the table and wonder what this other person can do for me. The question is, *What can I do for them? How can I enhance their life? How can I give myself fully to them?*

If that sounds scary to you, and maybe even somewhat uncomfortable, I'm with you. Earlier I wrote about a "naked and unashamed" level of vulnerability that defines real romantic connection. This is that same level of vulnerability in action. One of the most familiar verses in all the Bible opens with the line, "For God so loved the world that he gave . . ." (John 3:16 NIV). To love is to give, and when I fully love and fully commit, I am fully open and give myself to this person I've chosen to love.

Hopefully, my partner will enhance my life and fully give herself in return, but there will be days when that's not possible. I keep going back to the story I used to open this chapter. I can see these two old lovers under a tree, one giving herself fully and the other unable to reciprocate, but that doesn't stop her from giving more and more. That's what true love does; it gives sacrificially and opens our lives to something beautiful.

Perfection Not Required

Before I started dating the one I have chosen to love for a lifetime, Jessica, I was really nervous about getting into another relationship. She's such a wonderful human being who loves God and loves others. That's what first attracted me to her. Yet I fought the attraction. Even though a couple of years had passed since my time in the reality television spotlight, being on those shows had created an unrealistic expectation within me of what "romance" looks like. My dates on those shows consisted of little things like flying off to Dublin, Ireland, and having dinner with my date in a castle. You know, the sort of dates everyone goes on. The fantasy level for those dates was off the charts. But now, without ABC, I didn't have access to a biplane and pilot to whisk us off on a perfect date in the desert, where a hot tub was conveniently waiting for the two of us. Outside of the television fantasy world, I no longer had any idea what a good date looked like, much less a perfect one like I'd want to arrange.

And yet I had met this amazing woman I couldn't stop thinking about, and I didn't know what to do. I felt like I'd set a certain standard on television, and I was sure she'd be disappointed if dating me outside of that world didn't live up to it. That fear left me frozen. Finally, I was sitting in a hotel lobby one evening, trying to figure out what to do, when I texted one of my buddies and told him my dilemma. He texted me back and told me that this new stage of life I was about to enter might not be as unexpectedly exciting or glamorous as the one before. He warned me that I might sit here worried and concerned about all these things that could happen, but he also assured me that it was going to be so much more fulfilling. "There's a whole new depth, there's a whole new type of excitement that awaits you," he wrote. "And yes, it's going to feel different because it's going to be different, but the life that you're stepping into has completely new opportunities for joy that you could never experience without that partner."

I sat there staring at my buddy's reply and a feeling of relief came over me. I'd been nervous about whether I could create an experience for Jessica that might measure up to what she'd seen on television. My friend helped me realize that did not matter. I didn't have to create the perfect romantic environment.

On top of that worry, though, I was hesitant to give up the single life I had come to enjoy. It's not that I was dating around. Honestly, I didn't date at all for the longest time. It's just that I had grown very comfortable in my own skin, and I didn't want to jeopardize that by falling back into old relationship patterns. I had a habit of becoming a relational chameleon, changing into whatever I thought the one whose heart I was trying to win wanted me to be. The more head over heels in love I was, the more I lost myself. My friend's text opened me up to the understanding that real love, real connection, doesn't wreck your life. It enhances it, even as you give yourself fully to it. I didn't have to become the perfect guy and take this girl on the perfect date to make a real and possibly lasting connection with her. My friend reaffirmed that I had permission to be myself.

I had fallen into the trap many of us fall into. We feel the pressure to be perfect and to create perfect, Instagrammable moments on every date. The quest for perfection ends up wrecking relationships before they can even get off the ground. And it's not just the pressure we place on ourselves. I've met people, both men and women, who are sitting back and waiting for the perfect person to come along—the person who checks off every box of their expectations. I know all of us have some boxes to check off when it comes to being attracted to someone romantically. That's not what I'm talking about. No, I'm talking about a checklist based on watching too many princess movies and rom-coms, a fantasy list that no human being can ever live up to. Instead of finding love, those waiting for the perfect man or woman to come along end up alone, often complaining that there aren't any decent guys or girls out there.

Long-lasting relationships allow others to be human, just as they give us the same freedom. We all have faults. If you are with someone long enough, you'll see every flaw. Everyone will eventually say something they wish they could take back or do something thoughtless and insensitive that will hurt you. You'll have arguments over nothing, or you'll be on the receiving end of an outburst when someone's tired and cranky. Couples whose relationships have stood the test of time understand this, and they keep choosing to love anyway. They don't expect perfection, which is a good thing because it's not out there.

Jessica and I have now been together for a while. It's funny, because the other night she hung out with several of her friends and they all

WHAT MAKES LOVE LAST?

started asking her about me. They didn't ask what I was like or what it was like to date me. Instead they asked, "How great is it to date Ben?" as if dating me had to be great because they'd seen my dates on television and mistakenly assumed that was the real me. Jessica called me later and told me that all her friends think I'm perfect. I laughed because that's ridiculous. I then asked, "Well, do you think I'm perfect?" I loved her answer. "No, not at all," she said. She's seen me at my best and she's seen me at my worst, and she loves me anyway. Just as I've seen her at her best and her worst and we're still together. I think we might be on to something.

Savor Every Day

The biggest lesson I've ever learned about making a romantic connection last comes from my parents. I've already written about how they've been married for thirty-seven years and counting. I've also already mentioned my father's brushes with death. When I first started writing this book, I called my mom just to make sure I had all my facts straight about the three times we nearly lost my dad. At the time I was working on chapter 3, which is all about the brevity of life. During that conversation my mom told me something that really took me aback. "For years," she said, "I have prepared myself in advance, *consciously prepared myself*, for my husband to die." When I asked her what that meant, she said, "I think I have, in a way, grieved your dad's death. I have processed that in my mind."

It wasn't just my dad's cancer before I was born or his heart problems that had him in and out of hospitals throughout my junior year of high school or even his latest coronary problems that brought her to this point. My dad's father died of testicular cancer when my dad was only two years old. When my father got his diagnosis of stage four Hodgkin's lymphoma, my mom had to think that history was about to repeat itself. My grandmother, my dad's mom, spent time in Warsaw to help my mom care for my dad. You have to remember that my mother was pregnant with me and had complications of her own five months in that put her in the hospital for a time.

My mom explained how, during that period, when they had no idea whether the cancer treatments would work and my dad might survive, she and my grandmother had some very open, very honest conversations. "My first question was, 'How did you do it? How did you keep going when your husband died and you had a young child?'" my mom told me. My grandmother told her how her in-laws distanced themselves from her because they could not deal with the fact that my grandfather had died at such a young age. She ended up having to move back in with her parents just so she'd have help managing life and raising my dad. But she made it. She kept going because she didn't have any choice. And now, while dealing with my dad's cancer wasn't easy for my grandmother, she was there for my mom, supporting her every step of the way and guiding her through the grief process.

Thank God my dad is still with us today, but that experience more than thirty years ago changed my parents' relationship. I think this is their key for making it work long term. My mom put it like this: "I have been thankful for the days I have been given with him, but I also know there's always this underlying tone of, at any minute, those days might be over."

I have been thankful for the days. That's the key. My mom and dad savor their time with one another. They do not take a day together for granted, because more than once they have come face-to-face with those days ending. Too many couples just sort of drift apart over time. Their interests go in different directions, or they allow having kids or pursuing their careers to become such a huge priority that everything else becomes secondary. Before they know it, they feel more like old friends from back in the day instead of lovers. I've never seen that happen with my parents because they not only choose to love each other every day but they savor each day as if it could be their last. I can think of no better way to stay connected for life.

CHAPTER 13

Moving Beyond a Painful Past

L ove doesn't always last, and when it doesn't, the resulting pain often makes us hesitant to ever love again. I know this from experience. A couple of years ago I went through a very painful breakup that left me hurting and confused and wondering if I just needed to take a break from dating for a while, maybe even forever. To make matters worse, the breakup became very public. I mean, very, very public, as in, the breakup was *the* most googled breakup event of that year. The public nature of it meant that everywhere I went, I found myself reminded of my love gone wrong. Even today, long after both of us wished one another the best and moved on with our lives and found new loves, strangers still ask me about her and why we broke up.

A lot went wrong in that relationship, which is why I need to share the story. Looking back today, I realize that if I hadn't lived through that relationship, I could never be in the healthy relationship I am in now. When we first broke up, I retreated from the public eye and nearly gave up on love. That isn't to say I did not date after my breakup, but I was closed off, which made penetrating my soul in a romantic way pretty impossible. Now I can see the beauty of what took place and how what once felt like the worst thing ever proved to be a turning point for good in my life. All it took was time, perspective, and the willingness to admit my failures and learn from my past.

As you've probably guessed, I am referring to my relationship with Lauren, the woman I proposed to on the final episode of my season of *The Bachelor*. After our season aired, the two of us went back into the public spotlight with our eight-episode show on Freeform, *Ben & Lauren: Happily Ever After?* The producers added the question mark because they sensed there was trouble in paradise. By the time *Happily Ever After?* came along, there wasn't a lot of joy left in our relationship. Tension and pain had taken its place. Neither of us was happy, but we were still doing our best to make the relationship work. We went to couple's therapy and counseling, yet no matter how many steps forward we took, it seemed something would hit us and we'd be right back to confusion and doubt. I think the hardest part was wondering how we ever got to that place. It certainly wasn't how we started.

I met Lauren for the first time when she arrived at the Bachelor mansion along with twenty-four other girls, all vying to be the one to receive the final rose. When we first met, I didn't know she'd be the one I'd choose at the end. We spent so little time together that night, and I met so many people, there was no way I could have known. I went into that night very excited about what the show might hold for me. Before we started filming, a lot of my friends let me know they were praying for me and my time on the show. They weren't all praying that

I'd find the future Mrs. Ben Higgins, necessarily, but that God would use my time on the show to accomplish something significant in my life. If that happened to include finding a life partner, how beautiful that would be.

However, from the start, one part of the experience was not beautiful for me: the breakups. Even on the first night, sending girls home did not come easily for me. After my experience on *The Bachelorette*, I knew exactly how the women who did not receive a rose felt. They weren't just characters on a television show. These were real people with real emotions. From the first rose ceremony to the last, someone was always going to go home disappointed. That's not to say I was such an awesome prize that I wrecked these women's lives by not choosing them. I know better. However, any time you experience rejection, it hurts. Your mind runs to all sorts of conclusions as to why you were not chosen. *Was I not attractive enough? Smart enough? Funny enough?* Ultimately, you find yourself asking, *What's wrong with me?* Sometimes we never get past that last question. I hated inflicting this kind of pain on anyone, much less twenty-four anyones.

The night before the final rose ceremony, I sat on my bed praying, "God, whatever comes of this, please allow it to be beautiful. Please don't let it become a dark spot in my life." The final day of the show had the potential to be both. On the one hand, I planned to ask one woman to marry me. But on the other hand, before that beautiful moment could happen, I had to do one final breakup with a woman I truly believed I loved. Through my years of watching the show, I'd seen other people switch from the breakup to the proposal with what appeared to be ease. Until I faced the decision myself, I never realized how emotionally draining it could be. In the past I'd always had weeks or months or even longer between breaking up with a serious girlfriend and entering into another committed relationship. Now I had less than a day. That should have been my first warning flag that trouble might lie ahead.

When I got down on one knee and proposed to Lauren on the climatic final moment of our season, I didn't feel impending trouble, only celebration and happiness. After thirteen weeks of exhilarating new experiences and lots and lots of hard conversations, I was exhausted. Doing the show is like living through a heightened version of all relationships, with months and years of experiences compressed into thirteen weeks, and you do this with twenty-five people, not just one. Still, I was excited. Lauren and I had decided we were going to spend a lifetime together with all the sacrifice and commitment that covenant demanded. Only after we left the show and started trying to do life together did I realize we didn't have each other's phone numbers. I didn't even know her middle name. We still had a lot of work to do to build a relationship that could last. Lauren moved to Denver, and we started the process of dating and figuring out our future together.

The breakup didn't happen overnight. Most don't. The first crack in the foundation took the form of mistrust, which had a lot to do with what happened on the show. We didn't watch any of the episodes when they aired, but we didn't have to. Everywhere we went, people asked about what they'd watched on that week's episode. The questions were not healthy for us. Even without the questions, we wouldn't have made it. As we got to know each other outside of the fantasy dates of *The Bachelor*, we both started to realize that this perfect fit wasn't nearly as perfect as we once believed. We had to work very hard at even the basics of our relationship. At times we had trouble talking. Day in and day out, something just felt off, not at all what two people who were supposed to be madly in love with each other should feel. Rather than admit we were in trouble, we both put our heads down and tried to make it work. Every relationship has patches where such determination is needed, but something felt wrong about having to work this hard so early in our time together. People kept asking us about a wedding date, but neither of us could think in those terms.

The longer we were together, the more we both knew this wasn't going to work. Admitting to myself that it was over wasn't easy. Neither was confessing it to her. By the end we were barely speaking. The breakup itself came over the phone. If you wonder how you can end an engagement with a phone call, believe me when I say that both of us preferred it that way. Neither of us needed another tortured, face-to-face conversation about our relationship. We'd had far too many of them over the previous two years. It was like our time on the show never really ended. At least, not the bad part.

When the time finally came to throw in the towel, doing it in a phone call felt far healthier for both of us. I was on my way to New York with my boss when Lauren and I had a brief conversation in which we agreed she would move while I was gone. It was the best possible solution for both of us. I think we were both so beat up emotionally that we were just glad the whole thing was done.

The Aftermath of a Breakup

Two days after the breakup, my boss and I were waiting to cross a street in Manhattan when I spotted Lauren on the opposite corner with one of her friends. I had no idea she was going to be in the city, and she obviously didn't know I was there. The moment I spotted her, I turned around and started sprinting down the street back the way my boss and I had come. I ran until I came to a cross street, then darted around the corner. I stopped and peeked around to see if she was coming after me. Instead of Lauren, I saw my boss. He had no idea why I had started running, so he took off after me. When he caught me, he asked, "What's wrong?"

"Is she coming?" I answered.

"Who?" my boss asked. Then we both looked back to see if anyone was coming our way. No one was. I was relieved. More than that, I was happy she had not tried to catch me. To this day I don't know if she even saw me, but that's completely beside the point. Whether she did or not, or how she reacted, is not something I needed to know. What I did know was that two days after ending an engagement with a woman I once thought I'd live happily ever after with, I was happier hiding behind a street corner in New York than making eye contact with her in a crosswalk. We'd made the right choice for both of us, but the fallout had yet to start.

When news of our calling off the wedding (which had never actually been planned in the first place) broke, people got into it. I was not exaggerating when I wrote earlier that my breakup with Lauren was the most googled breakup story of the year. The combination of *The Bachelor* and *Ben & Lauren: Happily Ever After?* meant strangers we'd never met had very strong opinions about who was right and who was wrong. Team Ben and Team Lauren camps emerged, filled with assumptions and criticisms about one of us or the other. I compare it to the way mutual friends take sides when any couple breaks up.

The difference for us came in that these mutual "friends" were members of Bachelor Nation, the fans who have made the show so popular. Complete strangers regularly came up to me and told me, "I'm with you, I'm Team Ben. She had no right to treat you like that." These people meant well, but frankly, they had no idea what had really happened. They blamed Lauren for everything and were angry with her, which upset me because I cared for Lauren even though we were no longer together. I still do. I only want the best for her and her husband and family. Team Lauren people also weren't shy about coming up to me. Some unloaded on me about all I'd done wrong. That felt pretty terrible, and already I felt terrible enough.

Even though Lauren and I had reached the mutual conclusion that the relationship should not lead to marriage, seeing it end still took a heavy emotional toll on me. After the trip to New York, I flew to Los Angeles where I crashed on a friend's couch for ten days. I barely moved. Every day I sat in sadness, hurt, and confusion, wondering how and why everything had gotten to that point. One of the enduring images from that period of my life came when paparazzi happened to snap a photo of me walking out of a Los Angeles grocery store, a pint of ice cream in one hand and a bottle of whiskey in the other. That photo is a pretty good picture of where I was in my life right then.

Time went by and I eventually got over the hurt and confusion of the breakup. Instead of going right back out there and dating again, I pulled back in order to focus on other things in my life. I spent a lot of time thinking through my relationship with God and making adjustments there. I settled into a pretty good place emotionally and spiritually. Then I left my job and devoted my time to other work opportunities that my time as the Bachelor had opened up for me.

Most months I spent more time on the road than I did at home, which was good for me. Staying busy felt like a really good way to get past what I'd gone through. But I couldn't stay busy forever. With time I realized I needed to work on myself. I thought through a lot of the questions that have filled this book. I also looked back on my failed engagement, not with regret, not with longing to get back with Lauren, but with a desire to learn. I never wanted to find myself in that position again. However, the only way to ensure not getting hurt or hurting someone was either to never date again or to allow the experience to shape me into a different, wiser man. I chose the latter.

Hope to Move Forward

I know a lot of you have been burned in the past. Unfortunately, to love is to risk getting hurt. In my experience, I don't know which is worse—to be the one who gets hurt or the one who does the hurting. Both have made me hesitant to pursue future relationships. The first because I didn't want to get hurt again. The second because I did not want to carry around the guilt and shame I felt when I hurt people by treating them badly. When my relationship with Lauren ended, I came away feeling both. I'd hurt her and she'd hurt me, and that was part of the scar I carried around afterward.

When a relationship ends, it's not just the hurt that rocks you. When you have fully opened your heart to another and allowed your life to become intertwined with theirs, everything just seems off when they're no longer in your life. You don't just lose love, you also lose the one you did life with. Many times you feel like you've lost your best friend. Now you find yourself with tons of time on your hands and no one to spend it with. You end up with far too much time inside your own head, over-analyzing every detail of the past relationship, beating yourself up for what you did wrong, nursing hurts over what was done to you. Neither is healthy. Both keep you from moving forward with your life.

On my last night on *The Bachelor*, I had asked God to turn my decision to break up with one woman I loved in order to propose to another I loved into something beautiful. Given the way things turned out, it would be easy to conclude that my prayer was not answered. However, I now see that the end result was even more beautiful than anything I could have imagined, because the story does not end with a breakup.

Today I am happily connected to a woman I will spend the rest of my life with. I asked Jessica to marry me shortly after finishing the first draft of this book. By the time you read these pages, we may well be married. We haven't yet set a date at the time of this writing because the whole world is under isolation orders due to COVID-19. As I sit back and think about my relationship with Jessica and how we arrived at this place, I can honestly say that our journey owes a lot to the pain and confusion I went through years before the two of us met.

Our favorite song is Cody Johnson's "On My Way to You." That song points out how all our past experiences bring us to the place where we are now. The breakup of my first engagement played a huge role in that process. It made me a better man and better prepared me for someone as incredible as Jessica. Only now am I starting to realize that my response to Jessica, my commitment to her, the way that I express love, and the way we work through difficult situations all owe a debt to the lessons I learned before.

When I walked through all the previous pain and disappointment, I could not see how any of it could be good. Now I understand how vital all of it was to the success of my relationships today, not just with my fiancée but with everyone in my life. The pain and scars of my past have the potential to prepare me for greater relational success today. Whether they will or not is my choice. I can either dwell on the past with bitterness, or I can let my past shape me as I walk into a better future.

All of us face this same choice. Failed romantic relationships cut deeply. The stronger the connection, the greater the hurt, and the longer it takes before we feel like we can walk upright again. But there is hope.

One of the biggest lessons I learned between the end of my first engagement and meeting the woman I will marry is how too often we look to another human being to fill some of the most basic needs within our souls. We feel unloved, and we hope we can find someone to love us and fill that space. We feel rejected, and we want the one we love to give us all the acceptance we will ever need. Life has let us down. People have disappointed us. We need to find someone who can restore our trust in people and give us hope that there truly is someone decent out there. More than anything, we feel broken and incomplete, and we want to find someone who will make us whole again. True love will be the cure-all for our lives, we think, and this relationship will serve as the be-all and end-all for all we ever wanted. We're unhappy and alone. We need someone to come into our lives who can lead us into the happily-ever-after for which we have been waiting our entire lives.

But true love was never meant to fill these needs. If I look to Jessica or my parents or my friends or anyone else to fill the most basic of human desires, I will come away disappointed. No human being can ever fix the brokenness within our souls and make us complete. If we look for a savior within a relationship, we will always be disappointed because we have assigned them a task that no one can possibly do. The worst thing we can then do is give up and move on and start the search for the perfect one once again who will check all the boxes and fill all the holes in our souls. It is an endless search conducted in the wrong place completely.

I'm not telling you to expect to be disappointed in the people who come into your life. I'm telling you to expect them to be human. You need to give them the grace they need just as you hope they extend the same grace to you.

All of us want to be understood. All of us want to be loved unconditionally. All of us want to be fully accepted just as we are, scars and all. All of us long to find one who will breathe life into our spirits and tell us that we are enough. All of us carry this same void inside ourselves. No human being can fill that void, but thankfully, they don't have to. There's someone else who is more than up to the challenge.

PART 4

NO LONGER ALONE

Reconnected with God

CHAPTER 14

Belief and Doubt

G od is real. I know that to the core of my being. However, at times all I can do is "want" to believe God exists. I pray that there has to be something greater than you and me. I also clearly understand that a desire for something to be true does not make it true. That is why I have many moments of doubt and confusion and moments where I wonder what this whole life is about. I feel like I'm constantly going back and forth in my head, wrestling with the pieces of life that make no sense or seem unjust. I constantly ask myself the familiar questions that have been asked for millennia, such as, *How can a good God allow bad things to happen to people?* and, *Why does this God who creates not allow himself to be more fully known and easily accessible?* Obviously, these are not the only two questions I struggle with. Many more rattle around in my head. My hope is that all of these questions will eventually lead me to a more complete understanding of truth. Curiosity and intrigue push us all to understanding. Truth needs to be understood. Truth needs to be discovered.

I do not pretend to be able to prove to you that God exists. Through my years of doubt, confusion, and feeling like God had left me, I spent many days and hours wrestling with this question. I cannot be the only one who has cried out constantly for God to show up in my life while wondering if he actually would. Even admitting this struggle feels somehow like the opposite of faith, as if I've wandered into a taboo subject real believers should never come close to. However, being completely honest before God and myself about my struggle has always opened the door through which God has entered my life. I cry for him to show up, and that's exactly what he does—every single time. His answers to my pleading have led me to the overly simplified conclusion (and incredibly unjustifiable short conclusion for the power of the statement) that, if you honestly pursue truth, truth will lead you to God. And I believe that truth will ultimately lead you to Jesus. I have experienced the truth of Jesus. I have prayed and cried out to Jesus. More than that, I've staked my life on him.

All of my wrestling matches with doubt and confusion have convinced me that, if God is not real, all we're left with is darkness and hopelessness. If there is no God, life has no point. Death leads to nothing more than nothingness forever. Those who die experience annihilation. They're gone forever. Thinking about it makes me fearfully shudder.

We need God.

We need hope.

My soul cries out to God, begging him to be real.

And yet . . . I doubt. I wonder if there really is anything beyond death. I wonder if my life really does have a purpose. I question whether there is anyone out there greater than me who has a plan that will make our existence make sense in the end. I have moments when I am afraid the very idea of God is nothing but wishful thinking for those of us who are too weak to accept that life is all there is and death is the end.

Through the course of writing this book, I've explored the stories of many people who have gone through some of the worst circumstances life can throw at them. They have all shared some type of faith in something greater than themselves. They've all faced the hard parts of life with a faith and hope that has truly inspired me. Yet in the quiet of my room, lying alone in my bed late at night, not knowing when my last breath will be consumed, I wonder if we've all just been duped.

Santa 2.0

When I was a young boy, I was told that Santa Claus was real. I watched movies about him, and I saw pictures of him everywhere during the Christmas season. People told me that if I was a good little boy, this same Santa Claus would bring me all sorts of great presents. So I tried to be good. My parents took me down to the mall, where I sat on Santa's lap and told him all the things I wanted for Christmas. When Christmas Eve rolled around, my stocking hung over the fireplace where Santa could find it and fill it up with presents. Before I went to bed—and I always went to bed early on Christmas Eve so that Santa could come to my house—we put out milk and cookies for him to eat as a snack. Then, on Christmas morning, I woke up early and ran into the living room, where I found my stocking filled along with gifts under the tree. Santa Claus offered me joy and comfort. He lived in a far-off place and cared if I was "good." Does that sound familiar?

One day life threw me a curveball. My very simple view of the world was crushed, and my greatest fear became true. I found out the whole Santa thing was a lie. Even before my parents told me the truth, I already had my doubts about a guy riding around the world in one night in a sleigh pulled by flying reindeer. The story always seemed a little suspicious to me, but adults I trusted told me it was true, so I believed them. After all, I'd met Santa at the mall, and even when I got old enough to figure out these guys weren't *the* Santa, someone still filled my stocking and put gifts under the tree. Shockingly, I learned my parents did that. It wasn't like they tricked me and something bad happened to me. Getting gifts was great. But I wondered why they thought it was a good idea to give the credit to someone who doesn't exist.

My parents told me about Santa. And my parents also told me about Jesus. My greatest fear is that one day I'll discover the joke is on me and Jesus is nothing but Santa 2.0. I have days when I'm just waiting for someone to break that news to me, days when the whole idea of God just seems crazy to me. I know this sounds like a really odd confession to make at the beginning of a chapter about reconnecting with God, but I have had moments when I've been shocked at the story I'm basing my life on. It just seems, dare I say it, *absurd*. At some level I think it would be much easier if there was nothing holding me accountable or giving me purpose or loving me well. Then there would be no big reason for life, and I could just go do whatever. Some days I wonder why I don't just throw it all away.

This isn't a merely intellectual exercise, either. While writing this book I've had weeks where I've woken up in the middle of the night in a pure panic over the question of whether God is real and whether this life means anything at all. Here I am writing a book about a message I am so prone to doubt. This book is the greatest project I have taken on to date, and I do not want it to be anything but truth-filled, yet I've also found myself in tears, weeping over the darkness I see in the world and the seeming pointlessness of it all. Even so, as I travel through this desert of faithlessness and doubt, something always pulls me back to God. When I'm pulled back, it's always beautiful. It is not always pretty, but it's always beautiful.

Without Doubt There Is No Faith

If you've never wrestled with doubt, God bless you. This chapter isn't for you. You don't need it. I wrote it for people like me who probably grew up in church because your family took you, but you have a thousand questions that you never felt like you could actually bring up in church without being looked down on. I grew up in a culture where it seemed that good Christians don't ask questions, at least not questions about things like a snake talking to Adam and Eve in the garden of Eden or a donkey talking in the book of Numbers or a whale swallowing a human and then spitting him out . . . alive. You're just supposed to accept all those things on faith.

Maybe you had faith at one time but you also wrestle with doubt. I know a lot of people who have walked away, not necessarily from God but at least from the church, because there's so little room for nuance and mystery and searching for answers without swallowing easy answers. Jesus intrigues; his story, message, and lifestyle connect with us. His love profoundly changes our hearts, yet, because of a few talking animals, or maybe a church that has made us feel shame, we leave in droves. The church system no longer feels healthy.

I also wrote this chapter for people who at one time were really into God. At one point in your life you had this great enthusiasm for him, but not anymore. I don't know what soured you on the whole God thing. A lot of people are put off by all the rules that get thrown at you. Rules feel unnatural, like they don't belong in this pursuit of God. Jesus said all the rules in the Bible can be summed up by two commandments that go to the heart of what it means to follow him: love God and love people. That's it. Love God. Love people. Yet most of us were told we had to do a lot more than that. If you really love God, you will vote a certain way and you will dress a certain way and you will talk a certain way. And then there are the rules about what you better not do. There are a lot of "don'ts" that get thrown at us when we say we love God. Way too many don'ts.

Or maybe you gave up because you saw things in this world and in this life that shook you and there was no way of explaining them away. I have felt that. It seems like every day there's another story of people dying in the most needless way. Just this week, while writing this chapter, two people died when an avalanche buried them and no one could get to them. Two women also died when their car slipped off of a ferry and fell into the water. These two women were in the middle of life, sitting in their car, talking and laughing, and all at once their car starts moving and they can't stop it and now it's too late. Of course, every day brings news of someone dying violently at the hands of another human being. Why do these tragedies happen every day? Why do pandemics show up every century or so and wipe out hundreds of thousands, if not millions, of lives? I have no explanation and yet, as a Christian, I feel like I'm supposed to make something good of them, to find joy and hope in the midst of this tragedy even when I don't feel any joy or hope. I just feel sad and angry and confused and disconnected from God.

I think this is why a lot of us throw up our hands and walk away from God. Trying to put a "churchy" spin on everything that happens around us wears us out. The Bible says that "in all things God works for the good of those who love him" (Romans 8:28 NIV), but a lot of us can feel pressured by this verse to look on the bright side of everything. To pull it off, you have to lie to yourself and tell yourself that everything is somehow good. It's not, and I can't tell myself otherwise. A few verses later the Bible says that we are more than conquerors in the middle of all the bad stuff that happens to us. I understand this verse is telling us that following God is not easy, and trusting in him doesn't mean everything is going to be wonderful. Yet I've heard people talk about this verse in a way that makes it seem as if I have to always feel like I'm more than a conqueror, even when life beats me down and I'm filled with doubts about the goodness of a God who would allow all the bad things in life to happen. I can't with integrity make that leap. I know I'm not alone. No wonder so many of us walk away. It feels sometimes that the reasons to doubt far exceed the reasons for belief.

I emailed my doubts to one of my friends who, at the time, was my pastor. This is the same friend who called me one day asking to borrow some of my faith. At the time I emailed him, we didn't know each other that well yet. It didn't take long for the two of us to grow close, and the way he responded to my doubts was a big reason. He didn't make me feel guilty for questioning God and life and the fairness of it all. Instead, he celebrated with me that I even had doubts because, in his words, that meant I was thinking, that I cared enough about my relationship with God to get brutally honest with him.

My friend didn't treat my doubt as a problem to be solved. On the contrary, he told me that you cannot have faith without doubt. It is impossible to have one without the other. His explanation doesn't mean that we are to stay in the place of doubt forever. As my friend explained to me, doubt is part of the process of coming to grips with the divine absurdity of following a God you cannot see. "Ben," he said to me, "all you can really do is say, 'Jesus, today I'm going to do my best to walk with you.'"

Seem too simple? Maybe for some the idea of just trying our best does not seem radical enough. All I can say is it worked for me, and there is a story in the Bible that lets me know I'm in good company.

In Mark 9 a man came to Jesus with his sick son. He had nowhere else to turn. The man pleaded with Jesus: "If you can do anything, take pity on us and help us," he said.

Jesus looked at him and said, "'If you can?' Everything is possible for one who believes." Sound familiar? *Believe and anything is possible.*

But the man was honest with Jesus. He said, "I do believe, help me overcome my unbelief!"

Jesus didn't rebuke the man for his doubt. Instead, he healed the man's son (Mark 9:20–29 NIV, my paraphrase).

I love this picture of faith and doubt walking hand in hand. The man desperately wanted to believe but doubt kept crowding in. Instead of rejecting the man for harboring doubts, Jesus did exactly what the man pleaded with him to do. That's really all I want to help you do through this chapter. The first step of reconnecting with God is not to conquer all your doubts. It isn't to accept everything you've ever been taught about God on pure blind faith without questioning anything. Instead, I hope you'll get to a place to pray the same prayer as the man in Mark 9, one that I've prayed myself: *I believe. God, help my unbelief.*

One Step at a Time

My journey through the desert of faithlessness continues to this day. It is not an easy journey. For the past few weeks my fight against doubt has been especially intense. No matter how hard I try, I cannot shut out the questions that opened this chapter. They wake me in the night, leaving me alone in the dark, tormented.

That my battle with doubt has grown more intense as I have worked on this book is not a coincidence. As part of the writing process, I've had to open myself up to see and to hear things as I try to explore the questions I want to share with you in these pages. I feel the weight of the suffering that is everywhere, the suffering we don't always see when we look at the world through the lens of selfishness and easy answers. I've found myself with moments of overwhelming sadness and despair and hopelessness, the reason for which I will explain in greater detail in a later chapter. Yet as I feel these things, I don't want to jump to the conclusion that God will make everything work out in the end. I need to feel the weight of the questions. I need to wrestle with the doubt.

And I do.

At first I hated the weight, but now I feel I need to experience it fully. Instead of hoping this weight will go away, I'm leaning into it, exploring it, letting it wash over me. Instead of asking when this weight will be lifted, I find myself asking why there is so much despair in my life and why I feel like I am carrying this weight of despair. Is it because it is true, that despair is the right way to respond? Or is there something in this despair that's calling me to look deeper and to see this struggle in a different way?

If my doubts are true, if the divine absurdity of God is nothing more than a fairy tale, another Santa Claus story, then despair is the right way to respond. I can tell myself that I am still a good person and I can make an impact on this earth, but why bother? Does any of it really matter if the moment this life ends there's nothing but nothing, like a dream you forget the moment you wake up in the morning? But if my doubts are a pathway to greater faith, I still need to feel this weight, for it leads to a place I need to travel.

Despair may at times feel like the appropriate way to respond, but it also never feels like the most natural or the healthiest. So I cry out in my despair for some answers, for an Answer Giver greater than me and you to respond. Yet in my darkest moments and loudest cries for help, a moment of peace washes over me that I cannot understand, a peace greater than anything I could have brought on myself. This peace comes over me and allows me to believe for maybe one more day or one more moment. That is how I can write this book, telling you I do believe. I will not be surprised when I wake up again in the middle of the night, filled with panic, filled with doubt, and the battle begins all over again. But I was never promised this would be easy, and I have never learned anything useful without difficult and painful experiences. Once again I will struggle, and once again peace will come and I will believe for one more day.

That's all I'm asking you to try. Over the next few chapters I invite you to lean into the doubt and the questions and search for answers and for the truth with me. I'm not asking you to do anything more than simply open yourself up to the possibility of God, and then see what happens.

For me, the weight of the doubt and the despair and the panic and the fear makes me feel so small that I have to cry out for something greater. I literally call out, saying there has to be more because I cannot do this on my own. Surely I am not the only one who has felt this weight. There must be others walking through this desert with me, saying, *God, please be there. God, please show up.* I don't want to live like this. I can't live like this forever. And God does show up. It's not always easy and the way in which he shows up is not always clear, but he does show up. Usually it is a subtle whisper reassuring me that it is all good. Just keep going, one step at a time.

I want you to take that step with me. Lean with me into the biggest questions we will ever ask on this earth: Where exactly are we going? What does this connection with God look like? Let's explore these questions together.

CHAPTER 15

Out of the Box

Since the beginning of time, human beings have felt this need to reach out for someone greater than ourselves. What some have simply called the "God-shaped hole in the soul" yearns to be filled. God is the one who put that hole there. He wants to connect with us. He isn't hiding. He's close. However, that hasn't stopped people from making all sorts of wrong assumptions about him.

Even with the belief that God is near, it is understandable that God is not easy to understand. Now, I don't want to get into a religious debate at this point. That's not what I am talking about. I'm talking about how people define God and add baggage to him that makes him more distant from us, unreachable, if you will. When the truth about God does not fit our own life, labels, and agendas, then we create a box and make others feel like God needs to fit inside the box of our liking.

We put God in a box and then place that box on the highest shelf we can find. If you want to get close to the box, much less open it, there is a list of rules you must follow. The box tells you that God can only be found in a church on a Sunday morning or at some shrine on the other side of the world. If you want to know God, the rules tell you that you can only find him by reading a certain book or by joining the right group or by voting for the right politicians. The God in the box is far away, hard to please, quick to judge, and quick to get angry. If you don't follow every rule exactly right, God in a box is quick to cut you off on a whim.

I have trouble believing that's what God is actually like, and I'm not alone.

During the time of the Bible, people also had a lot of different ideas about God. The most popular expression of God divided him up into a pantheon of gods and goddesses who were more like enhanced humans than gods, sort of like superheroes in movies today. Every god and goddess had temples devoted to them where people came and offered sacrifices. In Athens the most spectacular temple was built for the goddess Athena. You can still see it on top of the Acropolis today. In the first century the temple held a forty-foot golden statue of Athena. Smaller temples to various other gods dotted the top of the Acropolis and were also scattered all around the city.

The apostle Paul visited Athens at the height of its adoration of the various gods and goddesses. What he saw troubled him deeply. However, he didn't go around bashing people; he reasoned with them. That does not mean Paul jumped into an argument with anyone. In that day the people of Athens spent a great deal of their time discussing and debating the latest ideas. Paul joined in. Eventually he stood before the entire high council of the city at a place called Mars Hill. There he was asked to explain what seemed to the people in the city to be novel ideas about God. He said,

> It is plain to see that you Athenians take your religion seriously. When I arrived here the other day, I was fascinated with all the shrines I came across. And then I found one inscribed, TO THE GOD NOBODY KNOWS. I'm here to introduce you to this God so you can worship intelligently, know who you're dealing with.
>
> The God who made the world and everything in it, this Master of sky and land, doesn't live in custom-made shrines or need the human race to run errands for him, as if he couldn't take care of himself. He makes the creatures; the creatures don't make him. Starting from scratch, he made the entire human race and made the earth hospitable, with plenty of time and space for living so we could seek after God, and not just grope around in the dark but actually *find* him. He doesn't play hide-and-seek with us. He's not remote; he's *near*. We live and move in him, can't get away from him! One of your poets said it well: "We're the God-created." Well, if we are the God-created, it doesn't make a lot of sense to think we could hire a sculptor to chisel a god out of stone for *us*, does it?
>
> God overlooks it as long as you don't know any better—but that time is past. The unknown is now known, and he's calling for a radical life-change. He has set a day when the entire human race will be judged and everything set right. And he has already appointed the judge, confirming him before everyone by raising him from the dead. (Acts 17:22–31 THE MESSAGE)

I think Paul's speech is a great place to start as we try to see God for who he really is rather than the small-sized God people try to explain away and stuff into a box. Putting God in a box is a dangerous game that causes an excruciating amount of damage to people. It has no place in a world of finite beings like us. That's why I find Paul's speech refreshing. He doesn't use a lot of churchy verbiage. Instead, he starts where we all are, curious, wondering if there is one greater than us with whom we can connect, and then he explains what this God is really like.

God Made Everything

So who is God? Paul calls him the One who made everything and is Master over it. Debates over the age of the earth or the process God used to make everything only muddy the truth. Paul simply said, God made the world and everything in it. That's it. That's all that's important to know.

When you look around the world, you see God's handiwork. Psalm 19:1 says the "heavens declare the glory of God" (NIV), which means more than seeing something God made when you look at a night sky on a clear night far away from the lights of the city. When you gaze on the beauty of nature, something stirs inside you in response to the artistry of God. That's why you don't have to go into a building somewhere to encounter God. Just walk outside and look around. He's there. The sun shines, the moon comes up, the trees bloom, the birds sing, and the animals rejoice because God is there.

But God's work in nature didn't stop on the day he made it. Paul calls him "Master of sky and land." Other translations use the phrase "Lord of heaven and earth." The words *Lord* and *Master* aren't just honorary titles. They speak of the active role God plays in caring for everything that he made. He watches over his creation because he cares about it.

A long time ago there was a popular view of God which said that, after he made everything, he just walked away and let the universe work its own way out. That's not what Paul says here. God is not some detached observer but an active participant in the world around us, including in the lives of you and me. Jesus said a sparrow can't fall to the ground without your Father God noticing. I love what he said next. "So don't be afraid; you are more valuable to God than a whole flock of sparrows" (Matthew 10:31). The God who cares about sparrows cares about you. That's who God is.

The God Who Is Everywhere

God also doesn't live in something made with human hands. In other words, God can't be reduced down to one place. You don't have to walk through the doors of the right church to find him or travel to a holy place on some sacred mountain. Wherever you are, you can find God there. His presence creates sacred places all around us. We have the opportunity every second of every day to stop and notice.

Not long ago I spent a day with a group of my closest friends, talking through parts of this book. We laughed and we discussed and we listened and we ate and drank and just enjoyed being together. About halfway through our time together it hit me: the hotel room where we all sat in downtown Denver had become a sacred place because God was there in our midst. He hadn't just shown up. No, God had always been there. It was like he was waiting for us to recognize his presence. That's the idea Paul was trying to get across to the Athenians. God cannot be confined to one space. Wherever you go, he's already there.

I love this idea, but it also sort of stops me in my tracks. God isn't everywhere because he's spread himself thin around the globe. Listen to how Isaiah 40 describes God compared to what he has made:

> Who else has held the oceans in his hand?
>
> Who has measured off the heavens with his fingers?
>
> Who else knows the weight of the earth
>
> or has weighed the mountains and hills on a scale?
>
> Who is able to advise the Spirit of the LORD?
>
> Who knows enough to give him advice or teach him?
>
> Has the LORD ever needed anyone's advice?
>
> Does he need instruction about what is good?
>
> Did someone teach him what is right
>
> or show him the path of justice?
>
> No, for all the nations of the world
>
> are but a drop in the bucket.
>
> They are nothing more
>
> than dust on the scales.
>
> He picks up the whole earth
>
> as though it were a grain of sand. (Isaiah 40:12–15)

He "measured off the heavens with his fingers"? That blows my mind. This is why God cannot be confined to a temple or a church. When we connect with him, we connect with something that has infinite, infinite power and majesty. Coming to him requires a basic humbleness where we recognize we are not the greatest and biggest thing to ever walk this earth. He is.

He Needs Nothing from Us

Also, contrary to popular belief, God doesn't need us to run errands for him. Human hands can't serve his needs because he has no needs. There's nothing, absolutely nothing, we have to do for him to open up his arms to us. He is God. He made everything and he owns everything, and if he ever needed anything, he would just make it.

This means God isn't in the business of striking bargains with us. We have nothing to offer, which is one of the most freeing truths about God I've ever read. He doesn't need anything from us, which means he's not into making all sorts of demands on us.

I recently heard the story of a monk who spent a couple of decades living in a cave. He stood on one leg in prayer for so long, he ended up losing one of his legs. God didn't need him to do that. God didn't need to see such extreme levels of devotion before he'd accept that monk or anyone else. He wants nothing more than to connect with us, the people he made to know him. We don't need to bring anything. We don't need to do anything. No temples to build or steps to crawl up. All we have to do is open our lives up to him, and he does the rest.

He Made Us for a Reason

Throughout this book one of my consistent messages for you has been: You matter. Your life has value and meaning and purpose. Paul put it like this: "[God] himself gives life and breath to everything, and he satisfies every need. From one man he created all the nations throughout the whole earth. *He decided beforehand when they should rise and fall, and he determined their boundaries*" (Acts 17:25–26, emphasis added). That last line means you are not alive in this time and space by accident. God planned it. It's part of his character. He is the God who not only made the human race, but he also laid out when you would be here and how you would fit into his plan for this world.

That is why I can say you matter. God made you. He has a plan for you. That takes me from being an accident to a planned event with real purpose and meaning. Yet that raises another big question: If my life has purpose, what is it?

I believe the answer comes down to this: God made us to know him. He wants to connect with us. Listen to Paul's words: "He made the entire human race and made the earth hospitable, with plenty of time and space for living so we could seek after God, and not just grope around in the dark but actually *find* him. He doesn't play hide-and-seek with us" (Acts 17:25–27 THE MESSAGE).

God's greatest desire is that we would reach out to him and connect with him. The Bible calls God our Father, who loves us with a love greater than our minds can comprehend. Jesus himself said the greatest commandment of them all is that we would love God with all our heart, soul, mind, and strength (Mark 12:30). In the next chapter we're going to dig a lot deeper into how God loves us and what it means to love him back. For now, as we talk about who God is, we'll just start with this: God wants to connect with you. He's not hiding. He's not throwing up walls and barriers to keep you from getting too close to him. He wants to be close to you.

One of the biggest lies that comes from the attempts to put God in a box is the idea that getting close to God is really hard and something only the sincerest believers can attain. I've read stories of people crawling up mountains until their hands and knees are bloody, just to try to get close to God. That's not who God is. It may create a good story and it may show commitment to the cause, but God does not need a mountaintop for you to reach him. He is here with you now. He doesn't place outrageous demands on us that we have to fulfill to the smallest detail before he'll pull back the curtain and let us get close to him. James 4:8 promises, "Come close to God, and God will come close to you."

The whole story of the Bible is about people connecting with God in unbelievably personal ways. Here's what's so amazing about that truth: the story of God connecting with people didn't end when the last book of the Bible was written. There's no difference between you and me and people in the Bible like Abraham and Sarah and David and Peter and Mary Magdalene. The people in the Bible weren't superheroes. They were regular people. That's why the Bible includes the stories of how they screwed up. Yet their screwups didn't cause God to give up on them. Abraham lied about Sarah being his wife to save his own life. Sarah laughed when God told her she was going to have a baby even though she was old. David slept with someone else's wife, then arranged for her husband to die in battle. Peter denied Jesus three times, and one of Jesus' ancestors was a woman named Rahab who worked as a prostitute before God changed her life. If they could connect with God, so can we.

You and I can live lives that could be written about in the Bible because we can have the same connection with God they had. How do I know that? God made us to seek him. They had breath and lived this life just like we are living now. He was a part of their stories, and he is a part of ours. He's not playing hide-and-seek. He's close and ready to be found.

God Is Near

Despite the fact that we sometimes feel lost and far from God, God is not remote. He is near. "In him we live and move and exist," Acts 17:28 said in describing the closeness of God. The verse sounds like it's describing water for fish. He's not only near, he is so close that wherever we go, he surrounds us there. His presence completely envelops us.

Psalm 139:8–12 put it like this:

> If I go up to heaven, you are there;
> if I go down to the grave, you are there.
> If I ride the wings of the morning,
> if I dwell by the farthest oceans,
> even there your hand will guide me,
> and your strength will support me.
> I could ask the darkness to hide me
> and the light around me to become night—
> but even in darkness I cannot hide from you.
> To you the night shines as bright as day.
> Darkness and light are the same to you.

No matter where we go, God is close by. How close? He's so close that he speaks to us in a whisper (1 Kings 19:11–13). No one speaks with a whisper from a distance. Our culture might shout at us, selling us the lie that we constantly have to post and check our social media feeds and be at a high volume to show the world how great our lives are because that's where our value comes from. But God's voice comes as a whisper. It's quiet.

So even though he's close, his voice is easily drowned out by everything else in our lives, which is often what makes us think he's not right there with us. To hear him, we have to stop and quiet our spirits and ask him to show up. That's the only way you can hear him whisper that he's here and he wants to connect with you.

Too Big for a Box

The last couple of phrases in Paul's speech talk about idols of stone or gold. Living in America, I don't have a lot of experience with actual idols. Most pastors and Bible teachers I've heard talk about idols always use the word as a metaphor. Our jobs become our idols or our stuff becomes our idol or our desire to have people see us in a certain light becomes our idol. But when Paul made this speech, idols meant physical idols, statues of gods and goddesses people worshiped and offered sacrifices to. The idols were their gods, reduced down to a size and shape that was easier to wrap their minds around.

People still try to do that with God. We keep trying to make him smaller and less mysterious. That's how we end up trying to cram God in a box. I love how these last few lines of Paul's speech put it. God is now calling for radical life-change, Paul said. God calls for us to stop trying to reduce him down to our size and instead stand in awe of the majesty of this God who is so much bigger and mightier and mysterious than our minds can comprehend.

This is the God who wants to connect with you and me. How do we know he is who Paul said he is in this speech? God validated it by sending his Son, Jesus, whom people killed but God raised from the dead. The resurrection of Jesus—that's the proof. Those who heard Paul bring up the resurrection thought that idea was absurd, and it is. Divinely absurd. Yet it is there on the cross of Jesus that I most connect with God. A man rising from the dead is absurd, yet it shows me the amazing love of God, which I cannot get enough of and continues to draw me in.

CHAPTER 16

He Loves You More

A few months ago I sat down at my desk and began to weep. I couldn't help myself. Sadness overwhelmed me to the point that I felt confused and angry and hurt and completely disconnected from God. This book had a lot to do with it. When I first started writing it, I had friends whose stories I needed to include because their lives eloquently showed truths I had trouble putting into words. You've met my friends already. Their stories moved me, and I hope they moved you as well. But because these are real people, their stories have changed, and the weight of the changes has left me searching for answers I cannot find anywhere. Thinking about them hurts, but I need to feel that hurt, because it's nothing compared to what they and their families have gone through, beginning with Annie.

Annie is gone, and I can't get over it. She passed within a few days of my last text conversation with her. I can't stop thinking about her.

I knew her such a short time before she died, but the conversations I had with her keep running through my head. Most of our conversations took place via text, and I cannot bring myself to delete them. Reading them I see her smiling face and hear her hopeful spirit, but I can hardly bring myself to smile, and I feel so hopeless because of how her story ended. As someone who confesses faith in God, I know how I am supposed to feel about her passing. She made this huge impact in the short time she had on earth. Now I'm supposed to be inspired by her example and try to make an impact with my own life.

I am inspired, but I can't bring myself to be happy that her suffering is over when I can't stop asking why she had to suffer in the first place. Because of her cystic fibrosis, never once in her life did she get to take a deep breath. When I think about all the hope she and her family clung to with each new medical procedure that was supposed to buy her more time and maybe even something close to a normal life but didn't, I get angry because none of this is fair. *Fair* is not the right word. What was done to Annie and her family is flat-out wrong. But whom do I blame?

Some will say that there's no one to blame, that good people get sick and die and that's just how life is. The painfully insensitive, far overused, churchy answer is that sickness and disease are the result of sin in the world. The world is broken, and part of that brokenness comes in the form of diseases like CF, which took Annie's life. All through this book I've made the case that we connect through our pain and vulnerability. If that's true, and I believe it is, then sickness and pain actually serve a purpose, since our hurts and brokenness connect us and bring us together.

And yet . . .

I still can't stop thinking about Annie. She had such a positive attitude and so much faith. Her perspective on life was simply beautiful. She wasn't angry over the hand life dealt her. Instead, she did her best to make the most out of the few days she had. If you go back and reread chapter 2, you'll rediscover that I used her story as a challenge to all of us to live as she lived. Life is short and we are mortal, and we must make the most of every single day we have on this earth. Why, then, has her death shaken me so badly? Could it be that, when I strip everything else away, when I look for someone to blame for what happened to her, I can only come up with one logical answer that I can't bring myself to explore? The Bible says God is love. If that is true, if God loved Annie, why did she have to suffer through so much pain?

Avery also weighs heavily on my heart. As I write this, he's back in the hospital. He caught COVID-19 and, as someone whose immune system is compromised, his outlook is dim. I just talked with him, and he is a shell of who he was before he entered his hospital room. He is stuck full of needles and medicines. I don't know how long he'll be there or what's going to happen to him. Hopefully by the time you read this, he is out and living the life he's always wanted. He wants to travel and see the world, not live in a hospital room. Over the past year his life had opened up so much. He had a job he loved and more friends than he'd ever had before. The two of us talked often about how he wanted to start dating and experience love and relationships and all that they may bring, heartbreak and all.

Why, then, is he stuck back in a hospital room just as life started becoming fun for him? I don't get it. It's not fair, and it makes me mad. But at whom can I direct my anger? On whom can I pin the blame for what's happening to him? I come back to the same answer I had when

I thought about Annie's death. I don't really want to go there because it makes me question the one truth I was told I could always count on. And that's the idea that God is good and he loves us. How can God love us while still letting things like this happen?

Connecting Through Pain

I'm not going to pretend I can fully answer that last question. Lots of books have been written about it, including one by my coauthor. Instead of trying to give you the greatest theological answer that will settle this question once and for all, I'll tell you what has helped me make sense of this question. One of the common themes running through the entirety of this book is the idea that we connect through our pain and brokenness. We all experience pain in life, and that common ground can bring us together. That's true of our relationships with other human beings, and it is true of our relationship with God.

Faith in God does not make life easy or even easier. Jesus said, "Here on earth you will have *many trials and sorrows*. But take heart, because I have overcome the world" (John 16:33, emphasis added). Even though Jesus has overcome the world, we will still experience many trials and sorrows. So if God doesn't take away our pain, what's the point? How can he love us and not shield us from the bad things in life? Since he is God, he could. But he doesn't, because rather than take away our pain, God finds us there. He has experienced pain as well. If this is all new to you, you might have trouble believing that last sentence. How can God experience pain?

That's where Jesus comes in. Jesus is God's Son. He was literally

God in human flesh. When Jesus came to earth, he wasn't born into a life of luxury. He was born in a barn to poor parents who had to flee their home country to save their son from the king who wanted to kill him. Jesus' earthly father, Joseph, died when Jesus was younger than I am today. Jesus never owned a home; he roamed around teaching all over Judea, which also means he was homeless. He and his disciples often didn't have food to eat. More than once they walked through grain fields and ate what they could pick as they walked. That was their meal for the day. He connected with the marginalized and the poor because he was one of them. But that is all just the setup for the end. Jesus was put to death as a criminal for a crime he did not commit. As he hung on the cross he cried out, "My God, my God, why have you forsaken me?" (Matthew 27:46 NIV). Three days later he rose from the dead, but the scars from the nails remained in his hands.

God doesn't take away all our suffering when we connect with him. Instead, he finds us in our pain and brokenness. When we are at our lowest, he is there whispering that he knows how we feel. Romans 8:35–39 gives us this promise:

> Can anything ever separate us from Christ's love? Does it mean he no longer loves us if we have trouble or calamity, or are persecuted, or hungry, or destitute, or in danger, or threatened with death? (As the Scriptures say, "For your sake we are killed every day; we are being slaughtered like sheep.") No, despite all these things, overwhelming victory is ours through Christ, who loved us.
>
> And I am convinced that nothing can ever separate us from God's love. Neither death nor life, neither angels nor demons, neither our fears for today nor our worries about tomorrow—not even

the powers of hell can separate us from God's love. No power in the sky above or in the earth below—indeed, nothing in all creation will ever be able to separate us from the love of God that is revealed in Christ Jesus our Lord.

This lists pretty much everything that can make us think God has forgotten us. That's why this promise was given. When we experience the harsh parts of life, God hasn't let us down. He hasn't stopped loving us. Instead, he is in the midst of these problems, waiting to meet us there. Some would say he has already met us there and all we have to do is stop and wait and listen.

In the deepest parts of our pain, confusion, isolation, darkness, and regret, God is there. This is something my friend Matt learned from personal experience.

Matt's Story

Matt moved to Denver right out of college. He'd landed his dream job and at twenty-two was making more money than most twenty-two-year-olds. His role in the company should have been over his head, but instead he was excelling. Even though he'd been on the job less than a year, he was already one of the top performers in his division. Friends and strangers from his college days reached out to him regularly, asking about the secret to his success. They wanted his advice and he freely gave it. Life wasn't just good; it was awesome! His future looked set, and Matt couldn't wait to see where it might lead.

Then one day at the end of the workday, his boss called him into a meeting with human resources. The meeting felt less like a meeting and more like a police interrogation. The interrogators threw out a date and time from three months earlier and asked, "Do you remember where you were?"

"No," Matt replied, unsure what was going on.

Then they asked him about a local Mexican restaurant and asked if he could have been there. Since that was one of the primary places Matt took clients, as well as a hot spot for employees to hang out to talk shop, he said, "Sure, I could have been there."

"Do you remember what you ordered?" they asked.

A sick feeling hit Matt in the pit of his stomach. He couldn't remember exactly what he had on a day that didn't stand out as unique from any of the ninety days that had passed since, but he knew something was off. He told them he couldn't remember specifically, but if that day was like most of the times he went there after work, he probably had chips and salsa and maybe a beer.

Then they dropped a photo in front of him. It showed Matt from behind in the Mexican restaurant, his company laptop computer open in front of him. All at once Matt remembered exactly what had happened on that day. He and a coworker had wrapped up their day at the restaurant in question. Even though Matt had been there less than a year, he was consistently outperforming his coworker who'd worked there two years. Matt had sensed feelings of jealousy, but he didn't give it too much thought. That is, until now.

"We received this photo from an anonymous source. They informed us that you were sitting there, sucking down margaritas," the HR person told him.

Matt looked more closely at the photograph. There were four or five empty glasses on the table even though Matt was alone. The co-worker had unexpectedly excused himself not long after they arrived and left. Since Matt had stayed, no one had cleared his coworker's glasses or plate from the table.

"I had a beer, which is pretty standard," Matt said.

The HR people looked at one another. "Why don't you take the rest of the day off and come back in the morning. I think we can clear this all up by then," Matt's boss told him with a smile. Matt left, hoping nothing more would come of the conversation, but something inside told him he should be worried. That night he called the company COO, who told him everything was going to be okay. "You aren't going to lose your job over this," Matt was told.

The next morning Matt went into work like it was any other day. It wasn't. His boss called him back into Human Resources. "This meeting is now on the record," one said. "Why don't you tell us again what happened that night." Matt's story did not change from the night before. He explained how he had one beer and nothing more.

Matt's answer didn't matter because the questions were not asked to get to the bottom of what had happened on the day in question. HR had already made up their mind. They found Matt to be in violation of a company policy buried somewhere deep in an employee handbook regarding the consumption of alcohol "on the job." He was accused of being intoxicated during working hours, which was completely untrue. Even though he was not in the office at the time of the incident, according to the anonymous source, not only was Matt sucking back margaritas, he was also visibly intoxicated while wearing his company name tag and working on his company-issued computer. Since the photo was taken from behind, Matt's name tag would not have been visible even if he'd been wearing it, which he was not. Like his answers to their questions, that little detail didn't matter, because Colorado is an employment-at-will state. They didn't need any evidence to fire him. He was given the option of resigning and being escorted out of the building without even having the chance to pack up his desk or say goodbye to his coworkers. Just like that, he was out of a job.

Matt walked out of the building in a daze. He flopped down in the driver's seat of his car and tried to wrap his head around what had just happened. Nothing made any sense, and not just the fabricated story of him being drunk at work.

The move to Colorado nine months earlier had not come easily. When he first started looking for jobs right before graduation, Matt ran into one dead end after another. When he did land an interview, a job offer never followed. After a long series of closed doors, he started to wonder what was wrong with him that no one would hire him. Keeping a good attitude during the job search wasn't easy, especially after he broke things off with his longtime college girlfriend. He'd already put a deposit down on an engagement ring and had started thinking about how to do the perfect proposal. All at once there was no proposal to plan and no job to go to and, as far as he could tell, not much of a future.

Matt prayed a lot, but God said nothing back. All his life Matt had tried to do the right "God" things. Coming from a long line of pastors, he'd grown up in church and even served as a worship leader for his high school church youth group. He attended a Christian college and stayed active doing ministry projects, all to no avail. He felt depressed and adrift, as if no one cared, especially God.

A friend had helped him out of that hole with a simple challenge. He knew all Matt had gone through, and all the "good" works he was doing in the name of God. His friend asked Matt why he did the "God things" he was doing. "Are you seeking God and his kingdom, or are you just checking off boxes?" As much as he hated to admit the truth to himself, Matt knew the answer. He was checking off boxes, piling up credits with God in the expectation that God was going to do something good for him in return. His friend turned that script on its head. He challenged Matt to stop everything: stop applying for jobs, stop doing his various ministry projects, stop pleading with God to repair his relationship with his ex-girlfriend. Stop everything and seek God and his kingdom.

Matt did. For two weeks he did his best to stop all the activity, still his heart, and seek God. Once he slowed himself down, he discovered God had been waiting for him to slow down enough for God to catch him. A short time later Matt landed his dream job in Denver. It truly was an answer to prayer and seeking God's face.

Now that job was gone. As he sat in his car, Matt could not help but wonder why God had moved him across the country and given him the perfect job and teased him with an awesome life, only to pull the rug out from under him now. If Matt had done something wrong and cost himself this opportunity, he could handle that. However, he'd lost his job because of a misunderstanding and a possible setup by a jealous coworker. This was not fair.

Matt pulled out his phone and called his mom to tell her what had happened. His frustration with God poured out. "Why did God move me here, set me up for success, then yank it all away?" he asked her. He kept venting for a while before his mom finally said, "I don't know, son. I don't think God did this to you. Maybe this job wasn't the reason for your move. Maybe God just needed to get your attention and get you to Colorado for some other reason."

Over the next few months Matt thought about what his mother had said. He received three months of severance pay, which, along with his savings, gave him a cushion so he could take his time to find the right job and find himself a bit as a person. Unlike his first job search, interviews and offers came flying in, each one offering more money than he'd made at the job he'd just lost. However, something made him hesitate before accepting any of the offers. He turned them down, one after another. That didn't make any sense, yet he couldn't help himself. In the meantime, he started playing in the worship band at his church while also focusing on checking his heart to make sure he wasn't checking off God boxes again. He made a conscious decision to stop, wait, and seek God. That's all God was waiting for.

The rest of the story is pretty crazy. A job posted at Matt's church. One of his friends told him he should apply for it. Every time his friend mentioned it, his answer was the same: "No offense, but I work in an industry where I make a ton more money. Why would I apply for this?" But something told him he should apply, so he eventually did. He made it through the first few rounds of cuts, all the while still interviewing for jobs in his chosen field and turning those jobs down. Then the church scheduled a job interview for him.

The weekend before the interview Matt volunteered to play in the worship band for a youth retreat up in the mountains. Before the first session, he stood outside, rustling the kids into the lodge and trying to get them excited about the first session, telling them, "Get inside . . . this is going to be fun." The youth pastor, Andrew, walked up and asked Matt what he was doing. "I'm getting people in the door!" Matt replied.

"No," said Andrew. "What are you doing with your life?"

"Yeah, I don't know, man," Matt said, completely aware that

neither Andrew nor anyone else had any idea he'd applied for a job with the church.

"No, man, you're missing the point. Dude, you were made for this. You were made for ministry." Then Andrew added, as he turned to walk in the lodge, "Heed the call."

Matt froze. Literally. He could not move. It was as if his feet were frozen to the ground. He felt like his breath had escaped his lungs, and chills ran down his spine. Right then he knew why God had moved him to Colorado, and he knew what his next job was going to be. He knew this feeling was his "call" to ministry. He felt as if the scales had fallen from his eyes, making his true passion and purpose in life clear. If not for losing his job unjustly, if not for being challenged to stop and seek God, he never would have experienced this moment where God spoke to him. God's love had pursued Matt. Being fired slowed Matt down enough to be caught.

That's what God's love does. He loves you so much. All you have to do to experience it is to stop and let yourself be caught.

CHAPTER 17

What Does God Want from Us?

I opened this book with a story that, when compared to the other stories I've shared in this book, almost seems out of place. Not getting picked to be anyone's reading buddy at the age of seven doesn't exactly feel like a traumatic, life-shaping event. And it isn't. The course of my life was not set that day in Mrs. B's reading class. Finding myself all alone after everyone else had picked a partner did not cause me to see myself as an outsider. It only confirmed what I already felt about myself and still feel today.

My story begins in Mrs. B's reading class perhaps because it stands in such sharp contrast to the other side of my life. I felt like an outsider, but I grew up blessed beyond all measure with two tremendous parents who loved me dearly and went out of their way to make sure I felt their love every day of my life. My dad was lucky enough to have a great job, which meant I never experienced want. Both sets of grandparents lived close enough for me to know all of them well. If my childhood were a television show, it would look like one of those bland, black-and-white sitcoms from the fifties or sixties. My life appeared safe, but it wasn't as simple as it seemed.

I've shared several stories about nearly losing my father multiple times. There are other stories, some humorous, some humiliating, some hard for me to believe, even though I lived them—like the time a minivan traveling fifty miles per hour hit me as I walked down a sidewalk, sending me flying up onto a lawn where a group of girls were playing beer pong. There was the time I fell underneath the bus on my first day of school; or the time I got my head stuck in a walking bridge and had to be cut out by the fire department while bystanders watched; or the time a cop discovered a trunk stuffed full of toilet paper after I got into a car wreck on my way to TP a friend's house; or the time I had to sit out of my senior year homecoming football game due to a severe case of jock itch, and the local paper's headline read, "Ben Higgins Sits Out of Game Due to a Severe Rash"; or the time, after receiving a simple procedure called "varicocele removal," my testicle became as big as an orange and I had to walk through the halls of my high school with an ice pack, which I was forced to sit on for three weeks; or the time a show was made about me and two friends after we were part of one of the largest drug discoveries in Miami, Florida, history when we found kilos of cocaine while walking down the beach. I promise there are more stories to be told, but we will need to save those for another time!

Mrs. B's story stands out in my mind because of the way it confirmed how much of an outsider I've always been. The feeling that washed over me that day stayed with me and is, in large part, what motivated me to pour myself into sports all through school. I played basketball and football because there I was part of the team. Stepping onto a football field as the starting quarterback gave me a place to cover up all my social insecurities. In my naivety I assumed I'd go on to play college sports, then I'd graduate, find a job, find love, and live happily ever after.

Then sports were stripped away by one unexpected play and a knee injury that ultimately, because of the length of time needed to heal, led to my addiction to painkillers. When I lost sports, I lost my identity. I felt like even more of an outsider. College made those feelings even worse.

It didn't take long after walking onto the campus of Indiana University to realize I didn't have a lot to offer because my identity had been built on my short golden years in high school sports, and once you walk away from high school, no one cares about those stories anymore. Now I was strictly a student, and not a very good one. I didn't even know why I had gone to college except I'd always been told that's what you're supposed to do. Every other student, I thought, had a clear set of goals for life and knew exactly what they wanted to do as soon as they finished school. I felt much more adrift and out of place in this community of overachievers.

Fast-forward to my decision to appear on *The Bachelorette*. On my own I never would have applied to be on the show, but one of my coworkers decided, for whatever reason, that I needed to be on it. I had moved to Denver about a year earlier, and I didn't really know anyone outside of work, which is funny because one of my reasons for moving there was to get a fresh start and change the narrative of my life. I told myself I'd take up mountain biking or rock climbing and find community with others through those activities. But I found it's hard to make a fresh start when you are still the same old you.

Rather than become the king of outdoor sports, I spent most of my time either at work doing a job I hated or sitting alone in my apartment. What made my job even worse was the gnawing sense that I didn't deserve to be there. A friend of a friend had gotten me the job. It's hard to feel like you belong when you're only there because someone did you a favor. But if I hadn't worked at that job I did not feel qualified for, my coworker never would have signed me up for a casting call for *The Bachelorette*.

Days before taping started, I flew out to Los Angeles and was sequestered in a hotel. All the contestants had to arrive early for photo shoots and to fill out paperwork related to our appearances on the show. Most of the time, though, I sat alone in the hotel room, flipping through TV channels, wondering why they had picked me. I had free room service and could order anything from the menu, but I didn't order much. One of the producers eventually asked me if there was a problem.

"I'm so anxious, I can't get anything down," I told him.

"There's nothing to be anxious about," he said. "You're going to be fine."

I didn't believe him. Others can tell you how great you are a thousand different ways, but if you don't believe in yourself, their words ring hollow. I didn't believe I was going to be fine on the show. Two nights before I'd flown out to California, my best friend and I had been hanging out when I told him I was really nervous about going on the show. I expected him to give me some really encouraging advice in return. Instead he said, "Dude, no need to be nervous. You definitely will make it at least a week. There are some weirdos on that show!" All I could think was, *Great. Even my best friend thinks I'll be gone in a matter of days.*

When the first night of filming finally came, I got into the limo with four other guys and thought my friend had probably been overly optimistic. Looking at the other contestants, I was sure I'd be gone the first night. As it turned out, I was the very first contestant to walk up to the Bachelorettes (if you remember that year, they had two Bachelorettes, Kaitlyn and Britt) and introduce myself. The. First. One. To this day, if you ask the show's producers to name the worst entrance of all time, I would expect them to name mine. Guys have shown up at the Bachelor mansion dressed like penguins, and they had a better entrance than me. I had a girl show up for my season wearing a horse-head mask, and she made a better entrance than me.

I walked up and spit out a very nervous, "Hi . . . I'm, uh, I'm, uh, really, uh, excited, uh, to be here. I'll . . . uh, I'll see you inside." I wasn't nervous about meeting the Bachelorettes. The real problem was I could not quiet the voice in my head that told me the producers had to be thinking, *This is one of our guys? How'd that happen? He's just filler. We needed twenty-five guys, and we could only find twenty-four, so he filled a spot, but he's a joke. He doesn't belong here.*

Since I was the first guy to arrive, I was the first inside the mansion. I walked in and plopped down in the middle of the couch. My feelings of being nervous faded and were replaced by a feeling that had come over me many times in the past. I told myself that if I could just disappear into the background, if I held my tongue and didn't say any more than I had to and just blended in with everyone else, then no one would dislike me. Then maybe, just maybe, I'd get to hang around long enough to gain a good experience before someone figured out I really didn't belong and they sent me home. So that's what I did.

If you go back and rewatch the early weeks of that season of *The Bachelorette*, you'll notice I'm rarely on camera. I took a lot of naps and hung back as much as I could. I tried to laugh at the right jokes told by the right people, and when I had one-on-one time, I tried to make a good enough impression not to stand out as a bad dude. I never expected to "win" because the show is really not about winning or losing. Either you connect with someone or you don't. I only hoped to be around long enough to get the chance to figure out if Kaitlyn and I might be right for each other long term. (Spoiler alert: we were not.)

My plan rocked along just fine for a few weeks and several rose ceremonies until one of the producers pulled me aside from all the other cast and crew and said, "You know, Ben, I don't like you." I stared at him with disbelief. Who was this guy with his big curly hair and beard, decked out in a tie-dye shirt, a guy who was nothing like me and who had a completely different belief system and a totally different attitude toward life? Who was he to come up to me and tell me he did not like me? Before I could say anything, he said, "And do you know why I don't like you? It's because I don't know you." There was something about the way he said this that went beyond his words. He didn't say it in an accusatory tone. Instead, he said it like a friend, which we now are. He said it in a way that told me he saw right through me in a way that nobody ever had before. "Tell me why I don't like you, Ben," he said.

I don't know why, but his question destroyed the wall I had been hiding behind not only in my weeks in the Bachelor mansion but ever since Mrs. B's reading class. Over the next four hours I opened up and let everything out. I explained to him why I didn't feel worthy of being loved and how I didn't think anyone would really like me if they got to know the real me. I knew how to be friendly. I knew how to fit in. I knew how to be kind and how to show respect when it was due. But I didn't feel as though someone could sit down next to me and, if I let myself go—as I was doing right then with the producer—they could like me, much less love me. This was in spite of how much love my parents and grandparents and extended family had lavished on me all my life, I explained. Why I felt like this, I didn't really know, but I told him of the times when these feelings overwhelmed me. "That's why you don't know me," I said. "That's why nobody here knows me, because I am afraid that when they know me, that will be the end of it."

Something amazing happened during that conversation. Not only did it bond me to a man who is now a close friend, but the conversation also set me free. It set the stage for my confession to Kaitlyn a few weeks later, when I told her a shorter version of the same thing. I laid my insecurities and doubts about myself out in the open for her and for all the fans of the show to watch months later when that episode aired. I actually watched that episode with my mom and dad. I was so nervous, wondering what the response was going to be. To my surprise, the response was overwhelmingly positive. As the messages rolled in with people telling me how they could relate to what I'd said, I started to realize that the insecurity I'd held on to for twenty-five years was the exact thing that would connect me to others. Others shared my pain, and through that shared pain, we connected.

But that's not the end of the story. Through this experience, I made the decision to own my inward insecurity. I did not choose to love it or cling to it as my sole identity. Rather, I chose to own it as part of who I am rather than hiding from it. And when I did that, I found that my focus ceased to be inward on myself. I became free to look outward. I was free to look at others and truly love them. When people came up to me to tell me how much they appreciated what I said because it captured exactly how they felt about themselves, I didn't just thank them.

Instead, I asked to hear their stories. I cared far more about helping them step beyond the feelings of being on the outside looking in—I wanted them to be able to connect with others in a meaningful way. And the best way I found to do that was by listening without judging or jumping in to give advice.

In short, when I got honest with myself and with others and with God about the biggest struggle in my life, I found that what had once handicapped me became an avenue for me to make a difference in other people's lives and do something bigger than myself. I couldn't even see that possibility as long as I was turned inward toward myself. I couldn't see anything but me. But once I stepped out of that place of thinking I was the only outsider looking in at a party I'd never be invited to, my eyes were opened to see the crowd of hurting people all around me.

In that moment I finally understood what Jesus meant when he uttered these words: "I am giving you a new commandment: Love each other. Just as I have loved you, you should love each other" (John 13:34). To love God means to love other people just like he loves me. And Jesus loves me and he loves you by connecting to us in our pain. He was the ultimate outsider. The Bible calls him a man of sorrow, someone deeply acquainted with grief. It uses words like *despised* and *rejected* to describe how people treated him (Isaiah 53:3). Jesus' story includes his best friend denying he even knew him while one of his disciples sold him out to people who wanted to kill him. When he needed his friends the most, they all ran away. Even the religious leaders, who should have welcomed him with open arms, rejected him and worked against him. Jesus was an outsider and he loved outsiders.

Now the only thing Jesus asks of me, his one new commandment, is to love others like he loves them. I never really got it. I never knew what that was supposed to look like until God put me on a reality show and had one of the producers gently confront me, which then led to me getting honest with myself in front of a national television audience. As humorous as you may find it, the journey that began in Mrs. B's reading class came full circle on *The Bachelorette*. It took all of that for me to see I was not alone in plain sight. I may have still been an outsider, but I was not the only one.

Now, instead of focusing on myself and my own feelings of inadequacy, I felt the gentle nudge of God pushing me to love like he loves. Not only did my journey now make sense, but the hurts along the way felt worth it. Today, I own them. I embrace them, because through my hurts, my eyes are open and the call of God is clear. *Love me, Ben*, I hear him say, *by loving others*. That's all he really wants of me, and that's all he wants of you. That's all God wants from any of us. *Love me by loving each other the way I have loved you*, God says. As hard as it is to believe, it really is as simple as that.

This simple command of God is what ties together everything you've just read. All of us experience being disconnected at some point in our lives. Most everyone I know has struggled with feeling alone in plain sight at times. The journey back begins by reconnecting with yourself. That's just another way of saying we have to get honest with ourselves about where we are and why we're there. It also means not staying stuck in that place of only looking inward. Honestly admitting where we are then leads us to open our eyes to those around us so that we can connect with others. Our connection with others finds its ultimate expression by connecting with the God who made us and who loves us and who wants to express his love to us through the way we love each other. Even our romantic connections find their fullest expression through connecting with God.

Connecting with self, connecting with others, connecting romantically, and connecting with God are not four different connections we pick and choose from. All are tied together. All lead us into finding the best version of ourselves, together. The common link between them all is love. Loving ourselves. Others. Romantic partners. And ultimately God. A reconnected life is a life that loves not in words alone but in action. This is what it means to pursue a life worth living.

You are a community maker. You have the ability to take a step into connection right now. It brings you and this world no benefit if you wait for connection to come to you. Instead, go out and connect with others.

People need people to give up the labels and expectations placed on us by our upbringings, shame, guilt, or false narratives. You need to begin living the story that only you can write.

People need people who look them in the eyes and say, "No matter where you have been or even where you are going, you are loved."

People need someone who will give them space to be heard without being judged or without having "answers" shoved back at them.

People need people to connect with them at their darkest points, sharing their pain and letting them know they are not alone.

People need God to help them make sense of this life and breath that they have been given, no matter how quickly it can be taken away. To give them purpose and connection with something greater than themselves and show them what it truly means to love others.

In this life we may feel alone in plain sight, but none of us are. We can be here for one another. All we have to do is reach out. Know that you are seen, you are heard, you are loved. Now go and bring that to others. The world needs you.

Bonus Chapter

NOW MORE THAN EVER

For you, moving from chapter 17 to this one was nothing more than the turn of a page. For me, five years have passed. When I wrote the previous chapter, it felt like a crescendo. But the very last paragraph was more than just a conclusion. If it were a movie we'd have been huddled on the sidelines of the national championship game, the clock down to two seconds and our team down by one. I'd have looked each of you in the eyes, doing my best to let you know that not only could we win this game but I had no doubt we would win! Cue the music. Break the huddle. In-bound the ball. Make the pass. Take the shot. The ball drops through the hoop in slow motion as the buzzer sounds, and the crowd goes wild. This is the feeling I wanted to convey in the final paragraph of chapter 17. We may feel alone in plain sight, but none of us truly are. All we have to do is see one another and hear one another and love one another. The world needs us, and we are ready for the challenge!

Then came COVID-19.

I finished the final edits on this book right after the pandemic hit.

At the time none of us had any idea how long it was going to last, nor could we have anticipated the damage it would do. I'm not just talking about those we lost to the pandemic. I'm also talking about the even heavier toll it took on our relationships because of the distance and mistrust and anger it unleashed. I thought we lived in the most isolated and loneliest period of history *before* COVID-19. But compared to the pandemic's aftermath, in which we still live, the previous moment of history was filled with peace and love and harmony.

Today we are more disconnected from one another than ever, huddled together in ever-shrinking silos with those who think and act and vote and everything else like we do. It's not just that we live in little silos—we're lobbing grenades at the other silos. My prayer in writing this book was that every reader would feel less lonely and could become a bridge builder. But now we live in a time where bridge building is looked upon with suspicion, and bridge destroyers are hailed as heroes.

I felt an urgency when I first wrote this book. Today that urgency has grown into borderline desperation. We need real connection: with ourselves, with one another—even romantically—and especially with God. The question is how to make that happen in a world more divided than ever.

Look Left and Right

One of the perks of running a for-purpose company dedicated to contributing all profits to social causes around the world is that I am often invited to attend conferences focused on attaining similar goals. Sometimes I attend these conferences as a speaker, sharing the story of my coffee company, Generous International. Other times I spend all my time in a booth meeting the caffeine needs of those in attendance while trying to raise awareness about Generous. Either way, I get to meet a lot of interesting and influential people.

One of the most interesting people I've met is my friend T, who runs a large shelter in Atlanta for people without homes. T truly lives and operates in two worlds. In one, he spends his time with the people so many have given up on or, worse, could not care less about. Many of us try to pretend that world doesn't exist or try to make it go away without dealing with its root cause. T does the opposite. He's right there in the thick of that world.

But T also operates in another world that allows him to make a difference in the first one. He spends a great deal of his time with business and political leaders, raising support for the shelter. If not for the time he spends in the second world, his work in the first would not be possible.

I recently asked T a simple question: How can I care more? He shared several ideas, all of which were really good, but the one thing I remember most is a story he told me. T was on his way to his office, dressed for a lunch meeting with important donors, when he happened to glance to his left. There he saw a man sitting against the side of a building, head down, feet drawn in, almost like he was trying to make himself part of the wall. T walked over to the man, stopped, and said hello.

The man didn't move. Head down, feet drawn in, as if he hadn't heard T.

Never one to take a hint, T repeated himself. "Hello," he said.

The man barely moved but then said in almost a whisper, "Hi."

T then sat down next to the man, extended his hand, and said, "I'm T. What's your name?"

The man sat still long enough for the moment to be a little awkward before slowly raising his head. When he did, tears streamed down his face.

"Why are you crying?" T said.

"No one has asked my name in so long . . . I can't even remember the last time," the man said.

When I think of where connecting begins, I think of this story. There was an old television series with a theme song that said we all want to go to a place where everyone knows our name. My heart breaks to think that there are people out there whose names nobody knows. Even if that is not literally true, the feeling is far more common than we think.

The subtitle of this book is *Searching for Connection When You're Seen But Not Known*, but the search for connection is even harder for those out there who don't feel seen at all, much less known. What can we do about this? Making genuine connections begins with something as simple as looking left and right and seeing those who feel invisible, just as T saw the man on the sidewalk in Atlanta. Just look left and right. See the unseen. Even something as simple as asking someone's name can break down walls that took years to build.

For all of my adult life, I have regularly prayed and asked God to remind me to look left and right for the outsider. God has consistently answered that prayer, although I haven't always followed through—sometimes terribly so. A couple of months ago I was on my way to the gym for an early morning workout. The gym isn't exactly in what one might call the wealthiest part of town. Every time I go, someone stops me and asks for money, which is why I carry a box of protein bars in my truck. On this particular day the box of bars was on the edge of its expiration date. I knew I needed to give the whole thing away to someone soon. I pulled into a gas station near the gym and noticed a woman on her hands and knees, picking crumbs and scraps of food out of the dirt. Talk about a divine appointment!

I hopped out of my truck, the box under my arm, and started walking over to her. I was maybe fifteen feet away when she stopped digging in the dirt and turned toward me. The moment I saw her face I froze in my tracks. Then I immediately got back to my truck as fast as I could. Why, you ask? Her face was painted up as a clown, as clowny as a clown can get. I am scared to death of clowns. Yes, I'm in my midthirties, and clowns scare me as much today as they did when I was a boy. Maybe it's because my grandparents had a creepy clown painting that looked down on me whenever I slept over at their house. Or maybe the thought of someone painting their face to hide their identity from children has always creeped me out. Whatever the reason, I could not get away from her fast enough. And I've been convicted over it ever since.

As I've replayed that day in my mind many, many times since, I realize that what I really needed to do in that moment was to make her feel seen. I didn't have to sit down and have an in-depth conversation with her. My lifelong fear of clowns was going to keep that from happening. But I could have stuck around long enough to hand her the box of protein bars and say something as simple as "Have a nice day" without running off like a frightened child. Looking left and right for the outsider doesn't demand grand gestures. Jesus once said that something as simple as giving a cup of water to one of the least of these was enough. The point is to see the unseen and do something, anything, even if they are painted like a clown.

Generosity and Connection

After my experience with the clown woman, I continued praying that God would remind me to look left and right. I still carry a box of protein bars in my truck, and I still do my best to notice and interact with the people God brings across my path. I do all of this—but not out of guilt. I learned a long time ago that guilt is a terrible motivator. When guilt moves us to act, every interaction feels like checking off a task on a to-do list. Guilt never brings joy, because it's never satisfied. No matter how much we do, there is still an endless list of tasks left to check off.

Rather than acting out of a place of guilt, I always try to start from a place of gratitude. In other words, my starting point for looking left and right to notice the outsider begins with the understanding that nothing I have comes from me. Everyone I love and everything I have and every opportunity that's come my way are all gifts from God. The Bible calls this *grace*, and grace is the only hope for a disconnected, lonely, angry world.

Recognizing that nothing I have comes from me feels a little counterintuitive. When I work hard to obtain what I need and want, everything I have certainly feels like it belongs to me. I put in the hours and paid the price, and I put my name on it. However, much of what I think of as fruits of my labor are really fruits of circumstances over which I have zero control. Not to be cliché, but every time I travel to poorer countries, I think about how different my life would be if I had been born there instead of in Warsaw, Indiana. I've met so many remarkable people who never had the opportunity to go to grade school, much less college, like I did. It's like the Bible says in Deuteronomy 8:18: "Remember the LORD your God. He is the one who gives you power to be successful." In other words, nothing comes from me and nothing I have is truly mine.

The second part of the equation is equally counterintuitive. If nothing I have comes from me, then nothing I have is truly mine. When my grip is tight on what I have, I'm too worried about losing it to enjoy it. My whole focus is on protecting and preserving what I own. It's like a guy who owns a classic car, a car he's dreamed of owning his entire life, but he's so afraid someone might run into him or carjack him at a stoplight or steal the car from a parking lot that he never takes it out of his garage. He might as well own a 2001 Toyota Camry that he could drive without fear of losing it. That's how life is. God wants us to enjoy what he gives us. The entire book of Ecclesiastes is built around this message. Life is short and life is hard, but the ability to enjoy this life is a gift from God. And we can't do that when we're holding everything too tightly.

When we recognize, however, that nothing we have is truly ours, that it all belongs to God, we're free to hold everything loosely, which then sets us free to be generous. Generosity as a lifestyle is what leads to connecting with the outsider and with our friends and with our loved ones and ultimately with God. The tighter I hold onto that which isn't even mine, the smaller I become and the more distant God feels. But when I live generously, both my personal life and my relationship with God grow.

Gratitude. Generosity. Looking left and right for the outsider. This is the only way to truly connect and overcome our epidemic of isolation and loneliness.

The Left Hand Doesn't Know What the Right Hand Is Doing

Jesus said that everything God requires of us can be summed up in two commandments: love God and love people (Matthew 22:37–40). And 1 John 4:20 makes it clear that you can't do the first without doing the second. We love God most by loving other people. Looking left and right for the outsider, connecting with the lonely, living generously, and giving ourselves to others are ways we put love into action through good works. However, when it comes to doing good, we must guard ourselves against two traps that our basic human nature sets for us.

The first trap is when we start to think that the more good we do for others, the more God will do for us, as if saying hi to a person living on the street or giving them a protein bar will make God love us more. Falling into this trap reduces God from the Divine to a dad in a family sitcom. We've all seen the plot a thousand times. One child watches their sibling mess up and decides to kick it into extra-good mode to become Dad's favorite. That's not how God works, nor is it a formula that works very well for us. Doing more in an attempt to score points with God harms our relationship with him by making every interaction transactional. We do for God now and assume he owes us something in return. Then, when life takes the kind of turns it always takes in a world filled with hurt and sorrow, we end up disappointed and angry with God for not keeping his part of a bargain he never made.

The other trap human nature sets for us is when we put love into action less for the impact it will make and more for the recognition we hope to receive from it. This trap leads us to go out with a protein bar in one hand and a phone in the other so that we can post it on Instagram later. Then what we do matters far less than how we can show it off. The better you are at showing it off, the more people admire you and the bigger your brand grows. Even worse, the love we claim to share is nothing more than pity, looking down on others rather than looking across. When I get caught in this trap, it isn't long before I begin to see myself in a savior role for those I serve. Adopting a savior complex is toxic to every relationship, especially with the Savior himself.

I find it frustrating to live in a world where somebody sees an old lady stumble and their phone comes out even before they keep her from falling. But that's our most basic nature. Praise is addictive. To try to keep myself from falling into this trap more than I already do, I intentionally focus on living out what Jesus said in Matthew 6:2–4:

> When you give to someone in need, don't do as the hypocrites do— blowing trumpets in the synagogues and streets to call attention to their acts of charity! I tell you the truth, they have received all the reward they will ever get. But when you give to someone in need, don't let your left hand know what your right hand is doing. Give your gifts in private, and your Father, who sees everything, will reward you.

Not letting the left hand know what the right is doing means checking my motivations every day, as Paul wrote in 1 Corinthians 13, the love chapter, "If I gave everything I have to the poor and even sacrificed my body, I could boast about it; but if I didn't love others, I would have gained nothing" (v. 3). If Paul were writing today, he might say something like, "If I gave everything away and sacrificed my body, and had over a million views on social media and half a million shares, but I didn't act out of love, what good did it do anyone?"

Generosity doesn't just mean giving. It means giving myself without expecting anything in return, especially not recognition or even thanks, something I have to tell myself every single morning when I roll out of bed. I thought living out this truth was necessary when I was single. I had no idea how much more it would be needed after getting married.

Generosity and Connection in Marriage

I became a minor celebrity after appearing on a reality television show that is all about the search for the one, my soulmate, the love of my life with whom I was going to live happily ever after. As you read earlier, that didn't quite work out. There was a reason the follow-up show we filmed had a question mark after the words *happily ever after*. I doubted my then-fiancée and I were in for a happily-ever-after future. She doubted it too. And in the end, it didn't happen, which, as I've already written, was the best possible outcome for both of us.

I didn't date for quite a while after that breakup. Honestly, I wondered if the fairy tale, happily-ever-after, all-my-dreams-come-true kind of love even existed, much less whether I might find it one day. Then I met Jessica Clarke. Unlike on *The Bachelor*, I took more than thirteen weeks to pop the question. Much longer. Closer to three years.

Even then, we were engaged for over a year and still lived in different time zones. We took our time, because that was how the flow of each of our individual lives led us. The wait made our relationship stronger. Neither of us entered marriage in an attempt to fill something that was missing in our lives. I don't expect Jess to be the source of my joy or happiness or fulfillment as a human being. She can't do that for me, and I certainly can't do that for her, because human beings were not designed to play that role in one another's lives. Only God can do that.

I also didn't marry Jess for what she can do for me, and she didn't marry me for what I can do for her. Love is not expressed by taking but by giving through generosity. I have discovered that the starting point for a healthy marriage is the same starting point for everything else in my life. Anything I have did not come from me and is not really mine. This is especially true of the marriage relationship. This understanding frees me to lay myself down at the feet of my partner with both joy and unwavering trust. Earlier in the book I called this being naked and unashamed. That is the level of vulnerability true generosity in marriage takes us to, leading to joyful compromise that makes marriage work.

How does this look on a daily basis? When I was single I played golf with my friends three or four times a week. Not anymore. Does this make me a worse friend to my golf buddies as a result? I hope not. I'm still me, and I still value their friendship as much as I did before. However, because I put my relationship with my wife over my golf game, I play far less often as my priorities have shifted. Do I play less golf because my wife gets mad at me if I do? Not at all. One of the most effective ways to express generosity within marriage comes through surrendering the need to control the other person. Jess and I didn't get married to restrict one another. Rather, marriage has freed us to become the best versions of ourselves, and the best part is we don't have to do it alone. We both have the other standing beside us, encouraging us, holding us accountable, celebrating our wins, and mourning our losses. We both see the other as a gift to be treasured, not an obstruction or a burden.

Generosity also frees us from falling into the scoreboard mentality that causes so many relationships to crash. Scoreboards keep track of who carries out the garbage and who cooks dinner and who makes the bed and who does the laundry and who sweeps the floor and who drinks the last of the milk and who takes the last piece of cake and who fills the car up with gas or mows the lawn or does one of the thousands of little chores life requires. When we keep score, every time my wife hangs out with her friends, it better be balanced by my getting to play golf with my friends. The scoreboard also tracks clothes and cars and shoes. New for you better also mean new for me. Then, when we add everything up at the end of the day or the week or the year, the score better be tied. If not, for those with a scoreboard mentality, resentment sets in, and resentment is toxic to every relationship.

Approaching marriage with generosity means turning off the scoreboard and focusing on life together. Isn't that why anyone gets married in the first place? Generosity means I wake up every day excited to share my life with this person sleeping beside me. I love sharing the world with Jess, and she with me. Here's the coolest part of marriage: when I fail like I did that day with the clown woman, I still get to come home to my wife knowing my failures won't be elevated. Jess won't condemn me. Instead, she speaks truth to me in love and light. Rather than push me down, she reminds me that our failures don't define us. The best part is, I have the privilege of doing the same for her when she's down. We get to share our best days and our worst.

Generosity also means we communicate and regularly check on one another's wants and needs and desires and search for ways to be better partners to one another. Replacing all of this with a scoreboard mentality would rob the joy from this relationship for both of us. Scoreboards mean we are on opposite sides, opponents not lovers. For any marriage to work, we have to be on the same team, serving one another, giving ourselves to each other without worrying about being served. But I'd be lying if I said it was easy, especially after a baby enters the mix.

Generosity and Parenting

At the time of writing this, I have been a dad for exactly six weeks, which, of course, means I am an expert. I now know the secret to parenting: I have no idea what I am doing. None of us really do. Babies don't come with instruction manuals. We're all just trying to figure this out as we go along. The good news, at least for Winnie, is that at this point in her life, there's not a lot I can screw up. Most of my duties come down to holding her and changing her diapers and picking her up when she wakes up hungry in the middle of the night and carrying her to her mom.

Jess is the real hero. Everything Winnie needs to stay alive comes from her. Jess not only gave birth to Winnie and feeds Winnie through her body, she is also better equipped to calm Winnie, since our baby girl spent nine months in the womb listening to the sound of her mother's heartbeat. I try to stay attuned and fill in where I can, but if I had a parenting scoreboard at this stage of our daughter's life, I'd be behind by twenty points and the game has barely begun.

But generosity in parenting goes beyond the relationship between Jess and myself as mom and dad. Giving without expecting anything in return is the very definition of parenting. This is true love. As every parent knows when a child comes along, everything in your life gets tossed upside down. But the surprising thing is, you don't mind. In fact, I love it. I don't enjoy waking up in the middle of the night or surviving on zero sleep—it's a good thing I own a coffee company right now. Nor do I particularly enjoy getting pooped on or wiping spit-up off my favorite shirt. But this is clearly what is needed of me right now, and I am so thankful I have this privilege.

Winnie and I don't have long conversations, or any conversation for that matter. Again, as I write these words, she's six weeks old. However, I treasure our moments of connection as she lies on my chest, listening to my heartbeat. And I pray that she feels safe and loved and connected to me as well.

When I spend time with my daughter, I never think about what I'm giving up. These moments with her are some of the most special I will ever experience in life. I know I'm just getting started on this parenting journey. I understand how my days of changing diapers will quickly move into Winnie going off to school and making friends and going to sleepovers and learning to drive and being asked out on her first date. Someday she'll probably watch season 20 of *The Bachelor*. I hope that if she ever watches it she'll say, "Dad, you were so cool when you were young," rather than, "Oh my gosh, Dad. This is cringe!" (I know. A man can dream.) I guess what I'm really trying to say is, I understand my time with my daughter and any future children we may have is going to fly by. I don't want my selfishness to get in the way of my enjoying every moment as a dad to its fullest. My parents laid themselves aside and have modeled generosity to me my entire life. I pray I can live up to their example.

Being a parent keeps me humble and teaches me generosity. Holding my small daughter, I understand how fragile life truly is and how every moment we have is a gift. Again, none of what I have comes from me, nor does it belong to me. All of it comes as gifts from a generous God who loves me. How can I do anything less than express his love in turn to others through my own generosity?

Now Is the Time

As I close out this book once again, I go back to the prayer I prayed before I wrote the first word of the original manuscript. Then and now, my hope is that by the time you reach this last page, you will feel less alone and more hopeful. I pray that this book has opened you to the possibility of connecting with others and given you the tools for getting started. But I'm not going to give another sideline speech to try to spur you to move out of your silo and connect with yourself, others, and God. Instead, I offer only a word of caution.

Connecting with others takes effort. It's hard. Dividing ourselves into ever smaller groups is easy. And living generously comes only through determination. Selfishness comes naturally; loving others unconditionally demands dying to self. The opposite of this kind of radical, generous love is not hate. It's indifference, and that takes no effort at all.

My daily prayer for myself is that I will make the effort and the sacrifices to live differently, and I invite you to join me. When we look beyond the labels with which we cover ourselves, when we look past the hurts and the heartaches and the anger and everything else that divide us, all of us are just people who were created to live connected lives. We need one another, now more than ever. I believe to the core of my being that the effort is worth it. Do you?

Acknowledgments

To all of those who allowed their stories to breathe life and truth into the pages of this book. To all of those who cared for my soul during this journey. To all of those who listened to me blabber and process the chapters of this book. To all of those who pushed me to dig deeper, listen more, and love greater. To all those who are a part of this team, this would have never been done without you. Thank you. From the depths of my heart . . . thank you.

Recommended Further Reading

A s I've mentioned, I've been on this journey right alongside you, and I wanted to share some of the books and blogs that have helped shape my thinking in hopes that they might enrich your journey as well.

BOOKS

- *Everybody, Always: Becoming Love in a World Full of Setbacks and Difficult People* by Bob Goff
- *Love Does: Discover a Secretly Incredible Life in an Ordinary World* by Bob Goff
- *Falling Upward: A Spirituality for the Two Halves of Life* by Richard Rohr
- *Learning to Walk in the Dark* by Barbara Brown Taylor
- *Daring Greatly: How the Courage to Be Vulnerable Transforms the Way We Live, Love, Parent, and Lead* by Brené Brown

- *A Million Miles in a Thousand Years: How I Learned to Live a Better Story* by Donald Miller

BLOGS

- Humanity and Hope United Foundation, www.humanityand hope.org/journal.
- Walk With Bravery, www.walkwithbravery.com.

Notes

1. Dhruv Khullar, "How Social Isolation Is Killing Us," *New York Times*, December 22, 2016, https://www.nytimes.com/2016/12/22/upshot/how -social-isolation-is-killing-us.html.
2. Charlotte S. Yeh, "The Power and Prevalence of Loneliness," Harvard Health Publishing, January 13, 2017, https://www.health.harvard.edu /blog/the-power-and-prevalence-of-loneliness-2017011310977.
3. John T. Cacioppo, James H. Fowler, and Nicholas A. Christakis, "Alone in the Crowd: The Structure and Spread of Loneliness in a Large Social Network," *Journal of Personality and Social Psychology* 97, no. 6 (2009): 977–991, https://doi.org/10.1037/a0016076.
4. Rick Warren, *The Purpose Driven Life* (Grand Rapids, MI: Zondervan, 2002).
5. James H. Cone, *God of the Oppressed* (Maryknoll, NY: Orbis Books, 1997).
6. Brené Brown, "The Power of Vulnerability," TEDxHouston, June 2010, 20:13, https://www.ted.com/talks/brene_brown_the_power_of _vulnerability?language=en#t-705067.
7. Brown, "The Power of Vulnerability."
8. Taken from my cowriter Mark Tabb's book, *How Can a Good God Let Bad Things Happen?* (Colorado Springs: Navpress, 2008), 93–94. Used by permission.

About the Author

B en Higgins is best known from season twenty of ABC's hit series *The Bachelor.* The show led to an enhanced social media platform that he now uses to share what he is most passionate about with others—his faith, his hope for humanity, and his love of sports. In 2017 Ben cofounded Generous International, a for-purpose company dedicated to contributing profits to social issues around the world. Ben stays connected with his loyal Bachelor following with his popular podcast, *Almost Famous,* which he cohosts with his friend and former Bachelor contestant Ashley Iaconetti.

About the Writer

Award-winning collaborator Mark Tabb has authored/coauthored more than thirty-five books, including the number one *New York Times* bestseller and Mom's Choice Award winner *Mistaken Identity.*

His other *New York Times* bestsellers include *The Light Within Me* with Fox and Friends cohost Ainsley Earhardt; *A Promise to Ourselves* with Alec Baldwin; *The Unusual Suspect* with Stephen Baldwin; and *The Sacred Acre: The Ed Thomas Story.*